MARIANNE MAHN-LOT
*Translated by Helen R. Lane*

# *Columbus*

D1431522

Evergreen Profile Book 33

GROVE PRESS, INC.
NEW YORK

EVERGREEN BOOKS LTD.
LONDON

FIRST PUBLISHED IN THIS EDITION 1961. ALL RIGHTS RESERVED.

Library of Congress Catalog Card Number: 61-5531

*Evergreen Profile Books are published*

*in the United States by Grove Press, Inc.*

*64 University Place        New York 3, N. Y.*

*in Great Britain by Evergreen Books Ltd.*

*20 New Bond Street        London, W. 1*

*First published in France by Éditions du Seuil, Paris, as* Christophe Colomb

MANUFACTURED BY MOUTON & CO., IN THE NETHERLANDS

*Columbus*
*by Marianne Mahn-Lot*

## Contents

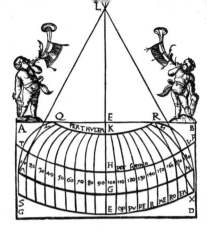

# THE YEARS OF APPRENTICESHIP

The supposed mystery concerning the birthplace of Columbus has now been resolved. Since the Genoa Exposition of 1892 (the 400th anniversary of the Discovery of the New World) the *Raccolta Colombiana,* edited by Cesare Lollis, has published an exhaustive collection of documents. The most impressive of these – the notarial records in particular – were republished in Genoa in 1931 in a folio edition, with accompanying facsimiles, entitled: *Christopher Columbus: Documents and Proofs of his Genoese Citizenship* [*Cristoforo Colombo: Documenti e prove della sua appartenenza a Genova*]. We can no longer question the existence of one Cristoforo Colombo, a native of Genoa, son of Domenico Colombo, a wool-weaver of the Ligurian coast. Hypotheses have been constructed around a Columbus born in Galicia, Catalonia, Corsica, etc.; he has been identified as a Catalan pirate named Colom or a Scandinavian mariner named Scolvus. Such hypotheses are mere fabrications, and are totally unwarranted.

There have been authorities who have gone so far, in fact, as to claim that the Cristóbal Colón who discovered the New World was not the same person as the Genoese Cristoforo Colombo. A book by the Peruvian

5

*The supposed birthplace of Christopher Columbus in Genoa, near the Porta Soprana.*

historian L. Ulloa, published in French in Paris in 1927 in support of this thesis, dismayed those scholars who lacked the tools to seize upon the weakness of his argument. His assertion – the result of a wildly hypercritical point of view – is completely untenable. The truth of the matter is that the Italian contemporaries of the Discoverer continued to call him *Colombo,* even though after his negotiations with the Sovereigns of Castile he signed his name as *Colón,* for reasons that were doubtless symbolic. One of the Genoese cousins of our hero was sometimes called *Giovanni Colombo* and other times (after he had joined his illustrious relative in Spain) *Juan Colón.* To put an end to these gratuitous discusssions concerning the homeland of Columbus let us cite one indisputable fact: the parallelism that exists between a Genoese notarial record of 1470, in which Cristoforo Colombo recognizes a debt he owes a certain Giacomo del Porto, and the codicil to the will of the Admiral of the Indies, in which the same person is named.

While admitting that Columbus was the son of the Genoese weaver, beyond all possible doubt, other historians maintain that he did not tell the truth about his birthplace, and are thus convinced that they are on the track of a great secret. In reality they are the victims of a certain negative bias, for we have no reason whatsoever to doubt Columbus' affection for his native land. No reason whatsoever, that is, unless his first will and testament, in which he states that Genoa was his birthplace, and enjoins his heir to establish in that city an annual income for a member of his family, is taken to be a forgery – a conclusion some authorities have not failed to arrive at, as we shall see later. No reason whatsoever, unless we totally neglect – as we cannot do – his friendly relations with Nicolò Oderigo, the Genoese Ambassador to the Court of Spain, to whom he entrusted a copy of all the royal certificates granting him privileges; his letter, dated April 2, 1502, to the Bank of San Giorgio in Genoa, in which he made the city of Genoa the beneficiary of one-tenth of his revenues from the Indies (a letter whose authenticity is now established); and, finally, the clauses in his last will and testament referring to Genoese friends. Since the Genoa Exposition of 1950-

1951 especially, when all these documents were put on public display, such facts are incontrovertible.

Salvador de Madariaga might thus have saved himself the trouble of basing a part of his argument in proof of Columbus' descent from Catalan Jews who had emigrated to the Ligurian coast on his supposed "lack of Genoese patriotism."

Let us examine for a moment this "Jewish hypothesis," which has enjoyed great success in France since publication of Madariaga's book. (Popular works present this hypothesis as an almost certain truth.) On the face of it, it might be tempting to explain Columbus' particular religious bent in terms of a Semitic ancestry. (Such an explanation must not, however, lead us to suspect the sincerity of his Christian beliefs, for it is obvious.) But not the slightest proof of such an ancestry can be brought forward, and in our opinion it is a total error to believe this to be a secret that Columbus carefully concealed, or the key to his personality and the mysteries that still surround the story of his life.

Partisans of this thesis (which goes back to Streicher, a German scholar) adduce, among other things, Columbus' profound knowledge of the Bible and of all the Messianic prophecies concerning Jerusalem. But every fervent Christian was acquainted with these texts, especially if, like Columbus, he was a lay-brother of the Third Order of Saint Francis, who read his office every day. As Columbus himself admitted, he was "not a cleric"; but a Biblical Concordance which doubtless aided him in his search for references has been found in his library. His passionate interest in the Bible is an important and persistent facet of his character.

This hypothesis has also been argued from the fact that Columbus was acquainted with Jewish scholars, and used their works. "I have had dealings and conversations with scholars of all sorts: Latin, Greek, Jewish, Moorish," he himself wrote. But this was true of any man of culture "interested in the secrets of the world" (the expression is his), for Hebraic learning was universally respected.

There is another so-called proof: the Admiral of the Indies used a mysterious cipher above his signature; this triangular sign is said to resemble those used by the Cabala. But if (as this argument would have it) Columbus feared that his Jewish origins might be discovered, would he not have avoided at all costs drawing attention to himself in this way? This cipher does, of course, betray a certain interest in the mysterious and the symbolic. But we must not exaggerate its significance. A man such as Raymond Lully (1235-1315), for instance, also took from the Cabala the habit of combining letters and figures; like Columbus, he was deeply interested in the Messianic promises attached to the name of Jerusalem. He was not, for all that, descended from Jews. . . .

This is Madariaga's reconstruction of the origins of Columbus: the great-grandparents of Christopher were a Catalan or Majorcan family named *Colom,* who fled the peninsula during the persecution of 1391, and settled on the Ligurian coast, where they adopted the spelling *Colombo.* But Genoese notarial records – which allow us to trace the family back to Giovanni, Christopher's grandfather, and outline the principal events of the life of Domenico, Christopher's father – furnish no sign of a Jewish background. *Domenico* and *Cristoforo* are first names that are undoubtedly Christian. Would Jews who had left their homeland in order not to deny their faith have established a line of Christian descendants so soon?

Madariaga's principal argument has a linguistic basis. It is quite true that Columbus, except for two short passages, never wrote in Italian; that as early as his stay in Portugal, where he settled when he was about twenty-five years old, he wrote either in Castilian (the first dated document: 1481) or in a Hispanicized Latin. The Spanish historian proposes the following explanation: the Colom family, after emigrating from the Iberian peninsula, continued to speak Castilian on the Ligurian coast, just as the Jews banished from Spain in 1492 kept Spanish as their language in the countries of the Near East where they settled. But Ramón Menéndez Pidal points out [1] that Catalan or Majorcan emigrants would have brought with them no spoken language except Catalan. Even if it were the case that Castilian was

---

[1] See *La lengua de Cristóbal Colón;* Buenos Aires, 1942.

spoken in the Colombo home, this Castilian would have had some admixture of Italianisms. The written language of Columbus does, in fact, show some Italianisms (his mother tongue being the Genoese dialect); but even more important, it shows numerous "Portuguesisms," so marked that only death will rid him of them: this indelible imprint is easily explainable if he learned Castilian at the Court of Lisbon, where Castilian and Portuguese were used concurrently. There is no reason, moreover, to be surprised that Columbus did not write Italian, a literary language he probably did not know when he left his homeland, where only the Genoese dialect was spoken.

There is nothing, therefore, in the "Jewish hypothesis" that should incline us to believe it. Its arguments can even be reversed. How does it happen, for instance, that in a country possessed of a Jewish phobia, as was the case in the Iberian peninsula during the reign of Their Catholic Majesties, the countless enemies of the Admiral of the Indies, who frequently denounced him as an avaricious and cruel foreigner, never accused him of belonging to the "race of the accursed?" The only evidence we have of such an insinuation is a phrase of Columbus' that has been wrongly interpreted.[1]

We do not maintain that it is impossible that Columbus had, through some distant ancestor, Semitic blood. What we do deny is that he felt that he bore a secret at once glorious and ignominious.

Through the parallelism of several documents, we now know that Christopher Columbus was born in 1451 in Genoa, probably just inside the Porta dell' Olivella. His father, a master-weaver and son of a weaver of the Ligurian coast, had married the daughter of a weaver of a village on the outskirts of Genoa, who brought him several buildings in the town as her dowry. The family lived in the capital of the Genoese Republic until the year 1470, when it settled in Savona.

This was thus a family whose social background was a modest one: in his *Commentaries* (1506) Antonio Gallo, Chancellor of the Bank of San Giorgio and long a friend

---

[1] See below, p. 146.

of the Colombo family, describes them as "plebeians." Ferdinand, the son and chronicler of the future Admiral, hinted, it is true, that an illustrious Roman named *Colon* had perhaps been one of their ancestors (!), that a noble *Colombo* family had tombs at Piacenza. The Admiral of the Indies no doubt allowed an aura of mystery to surround his modest antecedents; and, as Ferdinand says, "being very young, I dared not question him, out of filial respect." (Ferdinand was 18 years old when his father died.) Ferdinand himself enters a prudent disclaimer:

> There are some who would have me say that the Admiral was descended from an illustrious stock. . . . But for my part I believe that he was chosen by Our Lord to serve as a true Apostle; for it is on the shores of the sea and not in palaces that Our Lord chooses his Apostles. And thus, though the origins of the Admiral are obscure and uncertain, the destiny he proved himself to merit is the greater thereby.

A commentary which would not have displeased Christopher, the "Christ-Bearer," for Ferdinand also reports this proud declaration of Columbus:

> Let them call me by what name they will, for after all, David first tended sheep before becoming King of Jerusalem, and I am the servant of Him who raised David to that high estate.

Christopher was the eldest of three brothers and one sister. One of his brothers died at an early age, but the two others shared his fortunes, and the Admiral always showed great affection for them. He was a red-haired youth with a ruddy complexion, very tall and strong of limb, with blue eyes set in a long face with prominent cheekbones; the look in his eyes, at once piercing and reflective, was striking. (So he was described by those who knew him later; we have, unfortunately, no authentic portrait of him painted within his lifetime.) Until his arrival in Portugal at the age of twenty-five, the facts we have about his life are few; they suffice, however, to outline the main events of his early years.

10

Influenced, doubtless, by his humanistic biases, Ferdinand Columbus claims in his *History* that the future Admiral studied at the University of Pavia. Since Columbus was the son of a family of weavers, this seems wholly unlikely. (Furthermore, Columbus once wrote of himself: "I who am not a learned man. . . .") It is almost certain that young Christopher attended schools close to home in Genoa, where he learned calligraphy (Ferdinand elsewhere tells us that he had "a very fine hand, and could have earned his living therewith"), and the rudiments of geometry and cosmography – an education not at all uncommon in that great seafaring metropolis. Here too he began to learn the much esteemed trade of cartographer, in which he was later to excel. "I learned," he wrote, "the quickness of mind and hand to draw a sphere, and to project on it cities, rivers, islands, ports – all with their proper bearings"; he probably also received a smattering of Latin, an indispensable tool for cartographers, who translated the explanatory "legends" of their maps into this language. The demand at that time for accurate charts to fill the needs of navies and merchant fleets was great, and Genoa and Majorca represented the two great centers of cartography. Let us here briefly recall that the art of mapmaking arose in the thirteenth century, thanks to the use of the compass: knowing the bearings of a ship on the compass card and its approximate speed, it became possible to establish the relative position of two points. From this came the use of portulan-charts, atlases, planispheres marked off in rhumb lines. The first chart whose date can be established with certainty was a planisphere constructed by a Genoese, Pietro Vesconte, in the year 1260.

Until the age of twenty, Columbus engaged in a variety of complementary activities. He learned his father's trade, but practiced it only intermittently: he is referred to as a wool-carder [*lanerius*] in several notarial records; Antonio Gallo, the Genoese chronicler who was a friend of the Columbus family, says that Christopher and his young brother Bartholomew carded wool in their father's workshop, but that "as soon as they reached adolescence, they went to sea, after the manner of their people." (We thus learn that there may have been mariners in the family before.) And Columbus himself wrote that he "first went to sea at a very tender age": he was fourteen years old. In 1470 Domenico Columbus left Genoa and settled in Savona, where he had bought a tavern; while still practicing the trade of wool-weaving, he there began to sell wine and cheeses. Savona became Christopher's home port, and some of his early voyages no doubt included buying stocks of wine for his father's business.

He was soon caught up in the enormous bustle of maritime activity of the great Genoese maritime trading companies. The naval power of the capital of the Ligurian Republic, which had attained its peak at the end of the thirteenth century, had undergone a decline since Islam had seized the near East, but it was still very great. Genoa still had trading branches in the whole Mediterranean area: at Alexandria, Chios, Lesbos, Cyprus, and even in the North Sea (at Caffa), though their days were numbered and Genoa by 1475 had been driven out of almost all of them. Voyages were made to these ports to buy spices and alum, which were then traded to England and Flanders. The ships were out-fitted by private companies with an advanced capital structure, for it was private initiative that had made Genoa's fortune, and continued to be characteristic of the city. These great ship-owners – the Di Negro and Spinola families – were frequently to play a role in Columbus' life.

After the year 1473 – the last date that his presence in Savona is attested to in notarial records – Christopher appears to have chosen the sea as his calling once and for all. We know that he visited Chios, for he mentions it later in his shipboard journal; he probably did so in 1474 and 1475, as a seaman aboard one of the ships of the fleet outfitted by the Di Negros and Spinolas to search for resin and mastic on this island. Probably in this period also, he was connected with a powerful Genoese firm, the Centurione, whose commercial agent he later became in Portugal. The financial interests of this company extended from the North Sea to the coasts of Guinea and to England. Since gold had been declared the standard for all currency in the Genoese market, the Centurione, patrons of the Bank of San

12

*Port of Savona in the fifteenth century. (Pegli, Musée Naval).*

Giorgio in Genoa, were particularly interested in the gold mines of the Sudan.

Beginning with this period in his life, certainly, the horizon of the young mariner was not limited to the Mediterranean basin, for Genoese merchants in fact traveled regularly to England and Flanders, via the great port of Lisbon. Columbus could look out across the sea – that Ocean Sea whose admiral he would, one far-off day, become – and toward the south his mind's eye could look toward the shores of Africa, toward those ocean isles whose discovery pushed the limits of the known world ever farther.

His compatriots had long been interested in the lengthy voyage around Africa, for their Mediterranean trading branches were threatened by the advance of Islam. As early as 1291, shortly after the fall of Saint Jean d'Acre, two Genoese merchants, the Vivaldi brothers, had ranged the coast of West Africa "ad partes Indiae per mare Oceanum" ["to the regions of India through the Ocean

13

Sea"], for a tradition that had survived since antiquity (perhaps a memory of the expedition of Hanno the Carthaginian?) held that it was possible to reach the Indian Ocean by sailing around Africa. They had never returned. Beginning in the fourteenth century, more and more of the ocean routes toward the South had fallen into the hands of the kings of Portugal. But the Genoese nonetheless had a hand in the whole movement of discovery, for their reputation as navigators and cartographers caused them to be pressed into service by the Court of Lisbon. At the beginning of the fourteenth century a Genoese had been "Admiral" of the fleet of King Diniz. One of his compatriots who had followed him to Portugal – a certain Lanzarote – was the first to discover the far-off archipelago of the Grand Canaries (or at least one of the Canaries, which was named after him). In the year 1458, when Christopher was still a child, the Genoese navigator Antoniotto Usodimare had explored the Guinea coast for Prince Henry of Portugal. Returning to his homeland once his fortune had been made, he reported that he had met a white man along the Gambia River who claimed he was a descendant of survivors of the Vivaldi expedition! Another Genoese, Antonio di Noli, had discovered the Cape Verde Islands, the most southerly point of the known continent of Africa, and had obtained a slave-trade monopoly. Ocean navigation was beginning, thanks to the use of the compass and the adoption of fast caravels in place of heavy Mediterranean vessels. These caravels were rigged with a combination of square sails and lateen sails, for scudding downwind or beating to windward. Navigators now dared to venture far out from shore. Encouraged by the contracts offered them by the Court of Lisbon, they took possession of a growing number of islands: after Porto Santo and Madeira, occupied in 1420, came the archipelago of the Azores, much farther to the west. Flores, the island of the archipelago lying farthest west, was discovered in 1452 by the pilot Diogo de Teive. These islands took feverish hold of men's imaginations, for the land of the setting sun has always created a profusion of legends. Antiquity had situated the last resting place of the blessed in a distant ocean realm, the Fortunate

14

*The Canary Islands and the Isles of Saint Brendan.*
*(Detail from a world-map of 1367; Biblioteca di Parma).*

Isles. (It is quite possible that these were the Canary Islands, and quite possible that they had already been explored.) In the Middle Ages other legends fused with these pagan reminiscences, and marine charts bore their traces: from the fourteenth century, mythical islands are represented on them at varying points of the compass. Sometimes it is the isle or isles of Saint Brendan, who according to an Irish saga of the sixth century had sailed far westward to an archipelago which marked the portals of the Terrestrial Paradise. It was during a search for these islands that the Portuguese had discovered the Azores. Sometimes it is the island of "Brazil" ("O' Brazil" means "blessed land"), which Irish tales described as a place where gold dust and an unknown dye-wood essence lay hidden. But above all it was Antilia, also known as the Isle of the Seven Cities, which unleashed men's dreams and men's tongues:

16

The Portuguese have it that they peopled this island in the time of King Rodrigo [i.e., during the Moorish invasion of Spain]: seven bishops sailed off with their pastoral flock and settled there. They also tell that in the time of the Infante Pedro of Portugal [i.e., in 1447] a storm-tossed ship came to anchor there, and that the crew was taken by inhabitants of the island to a church where Christian rites were being held. . . . They add that several of the ship's pages picked up handfuls of sand and found it full of gold. [An account by Las Casas, the historian of the Indies.]

Hence the name Isle of the Seven Cities, there having been one city per bishop. The name *Antilia* probably derives from *Atlantilha* – little Atlantis – and may be a reminiscence of Plato's Atlantis, that happy kingdom swallowed by the sea.

Still farther west than Antilia (for naturally it was thought that the Atlantic Ocean washed the shores of both Europe and Asia) was *Cypango,* i.e. Japan, which Marco Polo had described in the account of his travels. The countless number of manuscript editions of the *Book of Ser Marco Polo* attest to the extreme popularity of the account of this Venetian traveler who at the end of the thirteen century had lived in China for seventeen years. Of Cypango, which in fact he had never seen, Marco Polo reported that "gold abounds there beyond measure," that the buildings had roofs of gold, and that "in the sea of Cypango there are 7,457 islands, of which there is not one which does not have aromatic trees and many sorts of spicery."

All this inflamed young Christopher's imagination, as he copied charts or listened to the yarns that could not have failed to reach his ears in the cosmopolitan world of the navigators. Ever after he was to "seek to know the secrets of the world. The art of navigation inclines one toward that," he later wrote.

Perhaps he was already interested in that land of *Cathay* (China) which was to become his obsession. The memory of it was far from dead in Genoa. Taking advantage of the tolerance of the Grand Khans of Mongolia in the thirteenth and fourteenth centuries,

17

Italian merchants – most of whom were Genoese – had traveled the routes of Asia in droves, building permanent settlements in the large cities. There were doubtless those who still remembered the Italian Franciscan missionaries who had penetrated to the heart of Asia, establishing a bishopric in Peking and relations with the numerous Nestorian communities still in existence. Marco Polo had spoken of the Grand Khan's desire to learn of the Christian faith. Saint Louis, and others after him, dreamed of an alliance with the Mongols against Islam. Since the establishment of the Ming dynasty in China in the middle of the fourteenth century, relations with the Far East had, it is true, been broken off almost completely. But the lightning advance of the Moslem Turks in the fifteenth century set men to dreaming once again of the providential aid that might be forthcoming from the mysterious Grand Khan. The arrival in Florence in 1441 of Nicolò Conti, who had lived for twenty-five years in Cathay, in India, and in Ethiopia (or, as these countries were called in the Middle Ages, the "Three Indies") was a great event. He was received in Florence by Pope Eugene IV, who was engrossed in plans for a crusade. At the same time, there arrived at the Papal Court a mysterious Asian Ambassador, "come from the regions of Southern India." The Ambassador boasted of the power of his sovereign and affirmed that there existed a kingdom of Nestorian Christians twenty days' journey from Cathay. The Pope's secretary, Bracciolini, who had held an audience with the Asian Ambassador, also set down an account of Conti's adventures that Conti dictated to him, which subsequently circulated in numerous manuscript editions. This was the latest news from Cathay, well calculated to arouse men's hopes. (The celebrated "letter of Toscanelli," which we shall discuss later, mentions these hopes.)

Cartography also benefited from the new knowledge of the Orient furnished by the voyage of Nicolò Conti, as is evident from the admirable world-map executed in 1459 by Fra Mauro of the Camaldolite Order (although admittedly it was a map which the city of Venice kept jealously to itself). From this new knowledge there also resulted a Genoese planisphere in 1476. But in drawing

18

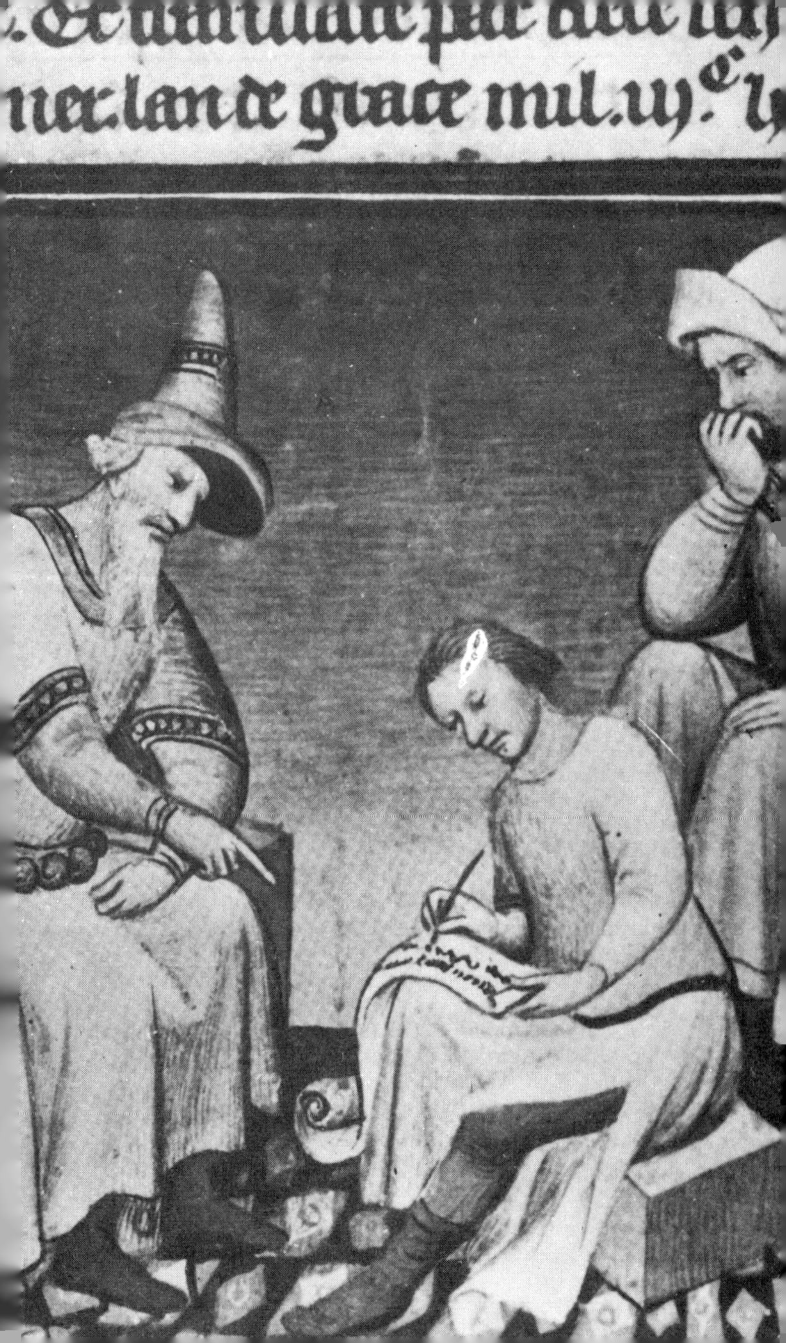
nee. lan de grace mil. iij.

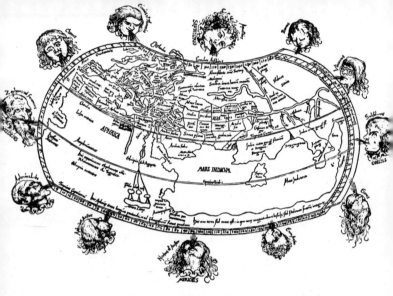

*The entire world, according to the* Geography *of Ptolemy.*

up their atlases cartographers still depended largely on the *Geography* of the Alexandrian astronomer Ptolemy (second century A.D.), although the first Latin edition of this work did not appear until 1406. In the *Geography* the measurements of the principal regions of the globe were indicated by latitude and longitude, but there were enormous miscalculations. The continent of Asia was represented as extending far eastward, its east coast thus falling close to Western Europe. Other cartographers exaggerated this extension of Eurasia even more, basing their calculations on the measurements of Marinus of Tyre, another geographer of antiquity. This is true of the Genoese planisphere of 1457, which the historian P. Revelli considers highly important. He concludes:

> Columbus found in the Italian charts of the end of the Middle Ages a representation of the Far West and the Far East which influenced his conception of the direct route to the lands of the Grand Khan.

For our part, we do not believe it was during his

Genoese period that Columbus conceived of the "mission" that was to be his: "to reach the East by sailing West," to open the Orient to Christian penetration. It was only gradually that this mission took shape in his mind, as he found support for his idea in the Latin compilations in which men of the Middle Ages had brought together the knowledge of antiquity, its Arabic revisions, and various scattered conjectures of the moderns. His mission was not conceived before the Portuguese phase of his life. Nor did it take shape before these treatises were printed, for Columbus, being a mere seaman, could not have laid his hands on enough money to buy them in manuscript editions. The invention of printing doubtless played a role in the discovery of America.

During these years of apprenticeship, which extend to his twenty-fifth year, it is above all as a man of action that the character of the future discoverer is forged. For even commercial navigation had its perils in those days. Monopolies were sought on all sides. The Venetians were the traditional rivals of the Genoese. The Aragonese and French fleets often engaged each other, for the House of Aragon and the Anjou dynasty were quarreling over the succession of the Kingdom of Naples, and the Genoese had thrown their lot in with the French contender, Prince René of Anjou. One of the rare proven facts we possess in this obscure period of Columbus' life is that he entered the service of this prince. Columbus later wrote: "It came about that King René sent me [from Sardinia] to Tunis to capture the galleass *Ferdinandina* [one of the ships of the King of Aragon]. . . ." He then boasts of having "altered the compass needle" – in other words, he magnetized its free end – to mislead the crew, who dreaded embarking upon this far-off adventure and wanted to return to Marseilles. Given the historical context, this year was surely 1472. And thus we find him master of a galleass, a quick-witted captain, and an experienced navigator at the early age of twenty-one.

In the opinion of competent naval historians, one of the most recent of whom is S. E. Morison, Columbus was one of the best navigators of all time. His dead-reckoning navigation was incomparable, but his theoretical knowledge was weak. We cannot, however, reproach him for not using celestial navigation, for at that time this was not one of the tools learned by apprentice-pilots; it was used only after landfall "to determine the latitude of the regions discovered in order to map them."

The Genoese phase of Columbus' life ends with a dramatic incident: a shipwreck off the coast of Portugal, an event in which Las Casas, the historian of the Indies, sees the hand of God – as is his prerogative given the providentialist point of view that is consistently his. The exact context of the shipwreck has puzzled modern historians, for Ferdinand Columbus, who had no direct sources, gave an erroneous account of it, which Las Casas subsequently followed. In the Italian chronicles of Sabellicus, Ferdinand found an account of the great exploits of a pirate named Coullon (whom he confused with his ancestor, the Admiral Coullon the Elder). During a battle off Cape St. Vincent Coullon had defeated four Venetian galleasses returning from Flanders. Ferdinand concluded that his father was a member of the pirate's crew and that the shipwreck had taken place during this battle. But as a matter of historical fact, the battle took place in 1485, and at this date Columbus had already ended his stay in Portugal. The whole episode becomes clear if we take into account another naval battle which took place in the same waters in 1476 and is known to us through the account of the Spanish chronicler Alfonso de Palencia and through Genoese documents. Early in August, 1476, a Genoese merchant fleet had sailed for England and had just passed Cádiz. Of the five ships, two belonged to the Spinola and Di Negro families (the same Genoese with whom Columbus had shipped to Chios). In spite of the French safe-conduct that had been provided the Genoese, they were attacked off Cape St. Vincent by Coullon the Elder, flanked by a task-force of thirteen ships. The battle was a bloody one, and the crews suffered a terrible slaughter. From this point we can follow the account of Ferdinand or of Las Casas. The ship on which the future discoverer was fighting had been bound to the enemy ship by a grappling-iron; a fire had then broken out on one of the ships and spread to the other:

22

[The fire] spread so fast that soon there was naught to do but jump overboard to die the faster; but the Admiral, being a strong swimmer and seeing himself two leagues or a bit more from shore, seized an oar that fate brought to his hands; holding on to it and swimming by turns, with God's help (for God was preserving him for greater things) he found enough strength to reach the shore, though he was so weak and exhausted that it took him several days to recover.

Ferdinand had no doubt heard his father's own account of this trial by fire and water.

And here begins a new phase in the life of the "Christ-Bearer."

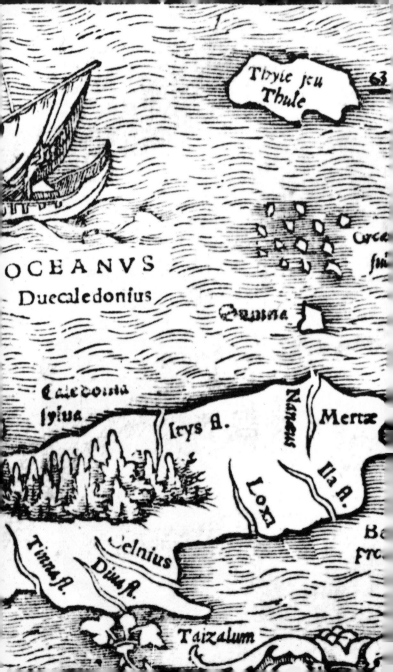

Thyle ſeu
Thule

Orca
ſui

OCEANVS

Ducaledonius

Caledonia
ſyliua

Irys fl.

Namets

Mertæ

Ila fl.

Lon

Be
fro

Tinna fl.

Diua fl.

Celnius

Taizalum

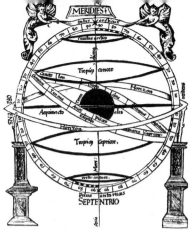

# THE GENESIS OF THE DISCOVERY

We have no direct sources for the period of nine years that Columbus spent in the Kingdom of Portugal, for the archives at Lisbon were destroyed in the eighteenth century. Details furnished by Ferdinand Columbus (based on his father's accounts and also on the latter's papers, now lost, which Ferdinand tells us he consulted), and the account of Las Casas, who questioned Diego, Columbus' elder son born in Portugal, are of some aid. We also possess notes written by Columbus in the margins of his favorite books; there are many of these, but it is difficult to determine which of them belong to this period.

Before settling in the kingdom of Alfonso V, Columbus had an adventure which throws an interesting light on his state of mind. This is the much-discussed voyage to Iceland.

From Cape St. Vincent, the site of the shipwreck, he went to Lisbon, which he had no doubt already visited, where he renewed his acquaintance with many fellow-countrymen, for members of the Spinola and Di Negro families were commercial agents in Lisbon for large Genoese trading companies. Two of the Genoese ships which had escaped disaster in the battle also made their way to the capital on December 12, 1476. They then set sail once more for England, to carry out the trading

25

*"I sailed beyond the island of Thule..." Detail from a map from Ptolemy's* Geography. *Note "Thyle seu Thule" at 63° north latitude.*

expedition so dramatically interrupted. We know that Christopher was a member of the crew on this voyage, and took advantage of the opportunity to push on as far as Iceland (via Bristol, and Galway, Ireland). In his father's papers Ferdinand found, in fact, the following statement, which he copied in his *History:*

In February of the year 1477, I sailed one hundred leagues beyond the island of Thyle; the southern part of this island is in latitude 73° north and not 63° as some would have it; nor does it lie on the meridian assigned to it by Ptolemy, which includes our West; rather it lies much farther west. To this island, which is as large as England, come English merchants, especially those from Bristol. And at the season when I was there, the sea was not frozen.

Learned scholars have long discussed this *Thyle* to which Columbus does not assign the same bearings as the *Thule* of Ptolemy. From Columbus' description of it, there is no doubt that it is Iceland; but when he wrote this note he emphasized how surprised he was to find that the island that he visited was situated farther to the north and west than the Thule marked on his own copy of Ptolemy's *Geography*. In the princeps edition of 1478, Thule is in fact represented as lying just to the north of Scotland, in the approximate position of the Faroe Islands. For the ancients Thule represented the northern limit of the known world (since Pytheas the Navigator had reached this land in the fourth century A.D.); the word thus had a lengendary aura. In the *Medea* Seneca had made this thought-provoking prophecy:

In the last years of the world an age will come when the Ocean will loose the bonds of things. An immense land will lie revealed, for a navigator will come, like unto the one named Tiphis who was Jason's guide, and he will discover a new world. And Thule will no more be the ultimate.

Later, after he had discovered this "new world," Columbus copied these verses in his *Book of Prophecies.*

26

He probably did not yet know of these verses in 1477, but already he seemed impelled toward the unknown. If, as he says, he sailed "one hundred leagues beyond Thyle," he may have gone as far as Greenland to the west or Jan Mayen Island to the north. Historians generally deny the possibility of such an extended voyage. R. Caddeo, an eminent authority on Columbus, ingeniously proposes that *oltra Thyle* [beyond Thule] is Ferdinand's faulty transcription of *a otra Thyle,* and that Columbus thus really wrote: "I sailed to *another* Thule." But if this is the case, how do we interpret the mention of "one hundred leagues"? It would seem to be certain that if Columbus had reached Greenland, he would have spoken of it in this note, rather than giving a description of Iceland. But in our opinion the possibility is not excluded that he did take this tack, however daring such a voyage might seem, especially at that season. A Danish historian, V. Steffanson, has established the fact that the winter of 1476-1477 was particularly mild, thus confirming Columbus' mention of an unfrozen sea.

We should recall at this point that Greenland was discovered in the tenth century by a Northman, Eric the Red, who sailed from Iceland; that a colony and a bishopric were established there; that Leif, the son of Eric (as has apparently been proven today), explored Newfoundland, Labrador, and a mysterious "Vinland" (currently identified as the region in the United States around Cape Cod). The Scandinavian settlements in "Green Land" declined in the twelfth century, but the memory of them was not dead, for at the end of the fourteenth century the Zeno brothers, who had settled in the Faroe Islands, sailed there and found traces of Christianity. (Their extraordinary adventures were not known, however, until the sixteenth century.) And in the year just past – 1476 – the King of Denmark had sent an expedition to Greenland with a certain John Scolvus as chief pilot. (The historian Luis Ulloa has made the wild surmise that Scolvus was Columbus!)

We may in any case agree with F. J. Pohl:[1] "From

---

[1] *La découverte de l'Amérique par les Vikings,* Paris, 1954. [French edition].

the tenth century the existence of lands in the West Atlantic was known in Europe, and at no time did this knowledge undergo a total eclipse." This fact played an important role in the genesis of Columbus' great enterprise: to reach the East via the ocean to the west. From this time on, this idea is ever with him, for he notes in one of his books that at Galway, Ireland, he saw two corpses washed up by the sea, and describes them as "men from Cathay" (Chinese); in reality, they were Lapps.

The legendary Irish tale of the isle of Brazil, a fabulous land where gold and precious dye-wood essences could be found, came to enjoy new popularity. It has been discovered that in these years seven expeditions set sail from Bristol for this mythical island. Beyond Brazil they sought to reach Cathay: reaching Canada twenty years later, John Cabot believed that he had found that land at last.

Upon his return from his Nordic expedition, Columbus took up residence in the Kingdom of Portugal, the center of a great movement of exploration which had been initiated around 1420 through the enthusiastic patronage of several remarkable Portuguese sovereigns, particularly the Infante Dom Henrique, known as Prince Henry the Navigator. The Pope in 1456 had granted the Portuguese sovereigns full jurisdiction over the coasts of "Guinea" (a generic term for all of Africa) and "all territory beyond leading to the Indies." The decree emphasized the religious hopes underlying the grant of so large a territory:

The Infante, mindful that within the memory of man the far-off shores of the Orient had never been reached by sailing through this Ocean Sea, believed that he would best give witness before God of his Christian zeal by rendering this Ocean Sea navigable as far as the Indies, which are said to bear allegiance to the Kingdom of Christ. Should he enter into relations with these peoples, he would move them to come to the aid of the Christians of the West against the Saracens.

28

*Prince Henry the Navigator and the future Affonso V of Portugal.*
*(Altar-screen by Nino Gonçalvez, fifteenth century, Museo de Lisbôa).*

*Caravan traveling to Cathay.*
*(Catalan atlas, sixteenth century; Bibliothèque Nationale, Paris).*

By these Indies "said to bear allegiance to the Kingdom of Christ" was meant the land of the mysterious
Prester John, a Christian potentate who had haunted the
imagination of Europe for three centuries – ever since
the arrival of a letter (which later proved to be totally
apocryphal) addressed to the Emperor of Byzantium. In
this letter the Priest-Potentate referred to himself as
master of the "Three Indies," lands of fabulous wealth
through which flowed one of the rivers of the Terrestrial
Paradise, and spoke of his desire to form an alliance with
the Christians to deliver the Holy Sepulchre. His capital
was thought at first to be in the Orient, where there still
existed numerous Nestorian Christians. But was it in
India proper, a land to which Saint Thomas the Apostle
had brought the Gospel? Or was it in the Kingdom of
Tharsis, the burial place of the Magi? Marco Polo had
spoken of royal descendants of Prester John in the Kingdom of Oengut, near the Great Wall of China. But
around the year 1439 Nicolò Conti, the Venetian traveler,
had reached the Court of Abyssinia, where he was re-

ceived by the Christian Negus. It was therefore supposed that the Priest-Potentate, weakened under the yoke of the Mongols, had had to retreat to "Third India," the name by which Northeast Africa was then known.

The economic aspect of the movement of exploration was also becoming more and more evident. In 1445 the Portuguese had reached the mouth of the Senegal River (which they took to be a tributary of the Nile), and thus a route was opened toward the gold-producing regions of Timbuktu. For centuries gold dust had been freighted overland to the ports of North Africa by caravan, the Christians realizing a profit from it only very indirectly, after paying heavy tribute to the masters of Islam. A small amount of the trade in this coveted metal was now routed through Lisbon, to the great envy of the other Christian nations. The African slave trade had also begun at this time.

By the time Columbus settled in Portugal, the movement of exploration had reached the Gulf of Guinea, and was so well along as to raise hopes that soon the Indian Ocean would be reached, thus opening the direct route to spice-producing lands that the Christian countries had so badly needed since the fall of Constantinople. (The spice route had never been completely closed; but trade, now entirely under Moslem control, had become increasingly precarious and costly.) The Portuguese advance had, it is true, come to a temporary halt, for King Affonso V, the reigning monarch, was engaged in a war with Castile and was faced with great financial and political problems. But Portugal's economic prosperity was nonetheless strikingly evident. As Morison writes:

Every spring fleets of lateen-rigged caravels, the type of vessel especially designed for this trade, were bringing into the Tagus bags of Malagueta pepper, cords of elephant tusks, coffles of Negro slaves, and chests of gold dust. . . . Along the quays and in the narrow streets of the old town all the languages spoken from Iceland to the Cameroons could be heard; seamen from Scandinavia, England, and Flanders jostled Spaniards, Genoese, Moors, Berbers, and converted Negro potentates.... Lisbon looked out and not in, forward to world dominion instead of backward to the glories of past centuries.[1]

Columbus probably settled in the Genoese quarter of the city. There he listened, asked questions, perfected his knowledge of Latin, and plunged into the study of cosmographic treatises. Since he had to earn a living still, he again took a post as navigator-agent for Genoese trading companies. In a document discovered in 1904 (the famous "Assereto" document, which is undoubtedly authentic) we find him, in August, 1479, momentarily in Genoa to settle his accounts with the Centurione company, which had sent him to Madeira to buy a consignment of sugar. And from this document it is quite evident that this visionary was a sharp accountant!

It was doubtless during this period that Columbus married. From Ferdinand's account we know that Columbus met, one day in Lisbon at the Convento dos Santos where he had gone to attend mass, Dona Felipa Perestrello e Moniz, a young girl whose noble birth had gained her entry into the convent's boarding school. Her dead father, Dom Bartolomeu Perestrello, had been the first Governor of the island of Porto Santo; her mother, Isabel Moniz, was related to the Braganças – in other words to the Portuguese royal family. "As he [Columbus] lived a most upright life and was a man of fine presence," Ferdinand writes, "Felipa esteemed him so highly that she became his wife." The plebeian antecedents of Columbus apparently presented no obstacle to the brilliant marriage. Isabel Moniz, it is true, was a widow of modest means, and her second daughter also married a commoner.

The marriage afforded the Genoese the best possible means of bringing his great enterprise to fruition. He went to live in Porto Santo, a small island just off Madeira, and it was there that his elder son Diego was born in 1480 or 1481: a fact attested to by Las Casas, who learned it from Diego himself. Columbus' mother-

[1] Samuel Eliot Morison: *Admiral of the Ocean Sea*, Boston, 1942; p. 32.

in-law is reputed to have handed over to him the documents and marine charts her husband Bartolomeu had left her. Las Casas writes:

> This pleased him much, and made his desire to study cosmography the more ardent. He thought more and more of this each day, and 'his imagination was set aflame.

One of his brothers-in-law, the Lieutenant Governor of the island, reported that westerly winds had once brought a plank carved by human hands to Porto Santo. Continuing his merchant voyages, Columbus gathered favorable omens from every corner and "noted them in writing in his books"; these Ferdinand later carefully copied. In the Azores he was told of large pine trees of an unknown species that had been washed up on the shores. (Even today the Gulf Stream carries plant debris from the Antilles to these islands.) On Flores, the island of the Azores archipelago lying farthest west, two corpses of men "with broad faces" had been found. A resident of Madeira claimed that each year he could see three islands toward the west; Columbus concluded that these were the Isles of St. Brendan. We should also mention, finally, the so-called Tale of the Unknown Pilot (a tale which began to circulate in the Indies early in the sixteenth century): Columbus was said to have taken into his house in Madeira a dying pilot, who told him that he had been driven by a storm to a distant island that lay far to the west, and furnished him with a chart and the bearings of the island. In all probability this was a legend, promoted by persons seeking to minimize the achievement of Columbus. Morison says: "It is impossible for a vessel to be 'blown across' the Atlantic from east to west. . . ." [1] It is even less likely that a ship in such condition could then have made the voyage home.

Columbus now extended his field of knowledge to the shores of Africa: from the frequent allusions he later made to the subject, we know that he sailed several times to "Guinea," going down as far as the Gold Coast,

---

[1]   Morison, *ibid.*, p. 62.

*The astronomer Alfragan. (From the* Compilatio astronomica, Ferrera, 1453).

where the Portuguese in 1481 had built their southernmost base, the fort of São Jorge da Mina. He maintained that at that time he often "took the height of the sun" with an astrolabe – an instrument that the Portuguese had developed for determining latitudes. He placed Mina in the wrong latitude, however, for he believed that it lay below the equator, having doubtless been deliberately misled by the Portuguese, who kept their secrets to themselves as a matter of policy. (Columbus does not seem to have known the *Manual of the Astrolabe,* which Portuguese scholars had just drawn up to serve as a standard table for celestrial navigation.) This experience in equatorial regions gave him the opportunity to note that "the torrid zones are not uninhabitable, as some say." During this period he also perfected his skill at navigation. As Morison writes:

> Columbus learned many useful things from his Portuguese shipmates, who were the world's finest mariners of that era: how to handle a caravel in head wind and sea, how to claw off a lee shore, what kind of sea stores to take on a long voyage and how to stow

34

them properly, and what sort of trading truck goes with primitive people.[1]

This trading truck – colored caps and hawk's bells – would one day bring Columbus enormous success in his dealings with "Indians."

It was in Africa that he also became acquainted with the slave trade, which ever afterward he considered to be a completely normal practice; having noticed the profits that the Portuguese earned from it, he was later to conceive the reprehensible idea of enslaving the natives of the "Indies."

Around the year 1483 Columbus' wife Felipa died. History has not permitted us to bring this feminine figure forth from the shadows that surround her, and she played no further role in the destiny of Columbus. Only one other woman was to appear in his later life; she too is a shadowy figure. "It pleased God to take his wife from him, for it was proper that for his great enterprise he be freed of all cares," Las Casas states frankly.

During the years that followed, Columbus was to attempt to further his project by enlisting the aid of John II of Portugal, who had ascended the throne in 1481. To this purpose, Columbus probably left the Azores to come to live in Lisbon, where he rejoined his brother Bartholomew, ten years his junior. Las Casas describes Bartholomew as "tall in stature, but less imposing," like Christopher a good navigator, with some idea of cosmography, and "greatly skilled, even more so than his brother, in the execution of marine charts." Bartholomew had a chartmaker's shop in the capital; he may also have sold printed matter, and no doubt his atelier was a sort of intellectual center. The chronicler Antonio Gallo credits Bartholomew with a decisive influence over his brother:

Bursting with tales of those who had returned from another world, so to speak, he shared with Christopher what information he had, and his conviction that a navigator who sailed westward would finally come upon a continent.

[1] Morison, *ibid.*, p. 42.

*Monastery of La Rábida (province of Huelva).*

With the close collaboration of his brother, Christopher thus spent his time in serious study and apparently abandoned all commercial activity; this would explain the debts he contracted in Portugal. He acquired the two books which for the rest of his life were to be his favorite reading: the *Historia rerum* of the humanist Aeneas Silvius, later Pope Pius II (1458-1464), printed in 1477; and the *Imago mundi* of the French cardinal Pierre d'Ailly (fourteenth century), printed around 1480. (These books have been preserved in the Columbus Library [Biblioteca Colombina] in Seville.) These he covered with "postils" – marginal notes – almost all of which were written in Latin. These notes are from different periods and are difficult to date; the earliest of these that we can date with certainty was written in 1481. It is also difficult to distinguish Christopher's notes from those in Bartholomew's hand. (Las Casas, who had these

36

volumes in his possession, is sometimes wrong; Christopher's "distinctive mark" is a small cross, which always precedes the notes that are his.) He had no doubt already read Marco Polo, for countless manuscript copies of the *Book of Ser Marco Polo* were in circulation in Portugal, and it was certainly this book that aroused his desire to reach "Cypango of the golden roofs" and the land of the Grand Khan. (Columbus' printed copy preserved in the Biblioteca Colombina is a later edition, however, which he bought in Spain after this period.)

Since he had been a mere merchant, a humble layman, Marco Polo was not an "authority" who could be invoked at the Court of Portugal – to which for several decades Prince Henry the Navigator had attracted a circle of eminent cosmographers and learned theoreticians. Like all men of his era, Columbus had to base his arguments on "authority": classic antiquity, the Bible, the Church Fathers. The *Imago mundi,* Pierre d'Ailly's lengthy treatise, provided him with this authority. This French cardinal's description of the world agreed with Aristotle's conceptions of the small size of the globe, thus heightening Columbus' instinctive impulse to sail west. In the striking phrase of one scholar, it was Aristotle who was responsible for the discovery of the New World [1] – the Aristotle who wrote in the *Treatise on Heaven and Earth* ascribed to him: "The region of the columns of Hercules and that of India are bathed by the same ocean." This was also the theory of Seneca and of Pliny the Younger. In the Middle Ages it was again taken up by Albertus Magnus and Roger Bacon. Against the followers of Ptolemy who believed in an immense ocean that could not be crossed, Bacon invoked the prophet Esdras: on the third day of Creation, God had dried up six parts of the globe; only the seventh part then remained under water. (This passage is from an apocryphal work, considered in Bacon's time to be a book in the Biblical canon.) There were thus many stretches of dry land. All these sources, as "digested" by Pierre d'Ailly, seemed to Columbus a convincing argument.

---

[1] Charles Jourdain: *De l'importance d'Aristote et de ses interprétations sur la découverte du nouveau monde,* Paris, 1888.

But unfortunately for him there was another currently accepted view of the dimensions of the globe, supported by the authority of Ptolemy, whose *Geography*, translated into Latin at the beginning of the fifteenth century with accompanying maps, was the basic cosmographic text of the time. Columbus acquired a copy of the first edition, printed in Rome in 1478. (His is a fine copy, with twenty-seven engraved maps, preserved in the Academy of History in Madrid.) Self-taught, he naturally respected Ptolemy; but on two points his opinion differed from that of the Alexandrian geographer – and doubtless it was for this very reason that he failed to impress either Portuguese or Castilian cosmographers.

Scholars had admitted since Aristotle that the earth was round (a fact which became widely known in the Middle Ages through Sacrobosco's *Treatise on the Sphere,* which after the invention of printing was circulated in many editions).

The terrestrial globe was divided into 360 degrees. But Columbus' first point of disagreement concerned the proper length to be attributed to a degree. For the school of Alexandria and Ptolemy, its representative, a degree measured 50 nautical miles; for the Arab astronomer Alfragan it measured 56 2/3 Arabic miles, i.e., 66.2 nautical miles. Columbus adopted Alfragan's measure (which was mentioned in Pierre d'Ailly), but wrongly assumed that the Arabic mile was identical with the short Italian mile: the degree thus measured 45 nautical miles, and from this premise the Genoese concluded that the world was 10 per cent smaller than Ptolemy had taught. His second point of disagreement: Ptolemy postulated that the known world – Eurasia – measured 180° from west to east. But an earlier astronomer, Marinus of Tyre, had calculated that it measured 225° (which would have made Asia fall at the actual longitude of Alaska). Pierre d'Ailly followed the opinion of Marinus of Tyre, and cited Aristotle, who had said that the ocean separating Spain and India was navigable. Columbus' long notes in the margin of these passage in the *Imago* attest to the decisive importance he attributed to such assertions. He writes for example: "The edge of the habitable regions to the east and the edge of the habitable regions to the west are fairly close to each other, and in the middle is a small sea." The "beginning of India" probably lay, in fact, not very far from the shores of Spain, since to Marinus of Tyre's 225° one had still to add, according to Marco Polo's estimate, 30° of east longitude to reach Japan.

It is likely that Columbus had already acquired some notion of these geographic conceptions in Genoa. (Paolo Revelli regards the Genoese planisphere of 1457, which follows the calculations of Marinus of Tyre, as a highly important influence.) They coincide exactly, moreover, with those shown on the celebrated Nuremburg globe constructed later between 1487 and 1492 (a reproduction of which is preserved in the Paris National Library). On this globe Cypango is shown in the approximate location of Mexico, on the same parallel as the Canary Islands (the parallel Columbus followed in 1492). This globe was the work of a German cosmographer, Martin Behaim, who had made an extended visit to Portugal from 1484 to 1487, where like Columbus he had married into a family of explorers. Columbus did not leave Portugal until 1485; he and Behaim may have met and exchanged points of view. Another coincidence: this same Martin Behaim returned to the Court of Portugal in 1493 (the New World had already been discovered, but the news had not yet reached Europe), and proposed an expedition to discover the Indies by sailing west. (This we know from a letter from the German astronomer Hieronymus Müntz to John II.)

We should here mention the celebrated correspondence between Columbus and Toscanelli, the object of heated discusssion among historians: it has been declared a forgery by H. Vignaud, accepted as genuine by C. Lollis, and generally considered authentic by recent scholars (by A. Ballesteros and L. Molinari among others), except for A. Cioranescu (in the *Revista de Estudios Americanos,* 1957) who believes it to be a letter "fabricated" by the Court of Portugal in 1494 (for reasons we shall discuss below). The correspondence consists of two letters from Paulo Toscanelli, an eminent Florentine scholar, who we know was interested in expeditions of discovery. The first letter has come down to us both in its original Latin form (as copied by Columbus on the end-papers of one of his books, the *Historia rerum*) and in a translation into the vulgar made by Ferdinand and Las Casas, who incorporated it in their *Histories;* the second letter is known to us only through these two biographers of Columbus. The circumstances and the tenor of the first letter are as follows: having been consulted by the Court of Portugal concerning the possibility of reaching the Indies via the west, Toscanelli apparently answered in the affirmative in a letter addressed in 1474 to Canon Fernão Martins of Lisbon, enclosing with the letter a chart representing the approximate distances between Spain, Antilia, Cypango, and Cathay. Once Columbus had arrived in Portugal, he may have learned of it through his relations at court. He may then have written to Toscanelli for more information, and obtained from him a copy of his letter to Martins and his chart. (What we have called the "first letter" is thus really Toscanelli's letter to Martins, with a cover letter addressed to Columbus.) Toscanelli's second letter, which bears no date but was naturally written before the Florentine's death in 1482, urges Columbus to persevere in his great enterprise. The scholar again emphasizes, as he had in the first letter, the importance of the enterprise to Christianity: merchants and travelers returning from the Indies have apprised him of the fact that sovereigns in that land wish to establish relations with the Christians.

Ferdinand and Las Casas assert that the encouragement brought by these letters had a decisive influence on him. But one mystery remains: Columbus never mentions Toscanelli, and it would appear that he never availed himself of the authority of the Florentine in his dealings with various sovereigns, for neither Columbus nor chroniclers of the time mention the subject. Certain historians have seen in this a deliberate silence, an attempt perhaps to conceal the fact that he stole the "letter to Martins."

In lieu of a detailed discussion of this debate, let us merely point out that the Toscanelli correspondence may not have played the decisive role assigned it by either the partisans or the adversaries of its authenticity. In his letter to Martins "Maestro Paolo" underlined the importance of the rich gold deposits and spices that lay hidden in Cathay, and the advantage to the Christians of reaching that land by the shortest possible route. All this was nothing new, however, to anyone who had read Marco Polo's account. But the fact that a learned scholar had accepted the descriptions and nomenclature of the Venetian traveler, who was widely read but generally considered to be a spinner of tall tales, nevertheless lent greater credibility to the *Book of Ser Marco Polo.*

There remains the question of "Toscanelli's chart." No trace of it has come down to us, but it is easy to reconstruct it from the description of it in the letter to Martins:

> From Lisbon to the most noble city of Quinsay [i.e., South China] there are 26 spaces, each measuring 250 miles...; from the island of Antilia, which you call the Isle of Seven Cities, to the great isle of Cypango, are 10 spaces.

The Portuguese coast was thus presumably 6,500 nautical miles (i.e., 250 miles multiplied by 26) from the coast of Cathay – i.e. 130 degrees (using the Ptolemaic calculation of 50 miles to 1 degree). Eurasia thus supposedly stretched out over 230 degrees (360 degrees minus 130 degrees).

If this chart did exist, did it play a decisive part in Columbus' conception? We have just seen that by combining the calculations of Marinus of Tyre and of Alfragan, Columbus had arrived at even more optimistic conclusions in regard to the short distance separating Europe from Asia. Had he projected his own estimates on the "sphere" that (according to Ferdinand and Las Casas) he sent to Toscanelli to indicate the tenor of his ideas? But did Toscanelli's chart really exist? Las Casas answers in the affirmative: he says that he has it in his possession, and identifies it with the chart that Columbus carried aboard the *Santa María,* on which were marked, he says, "all the islands and the mainland marking the beginning of India." But the historian of the Indies may have been mistaken: nowhere in his shipboard journal does Columbus say that the chart he consulted was that of "Maestro Paolo." Why would it not have been a

41

# MAP ILLUSTRATING THE GEOGRAPHICAL IDEAS OF COLUMBUS CONCERNIN

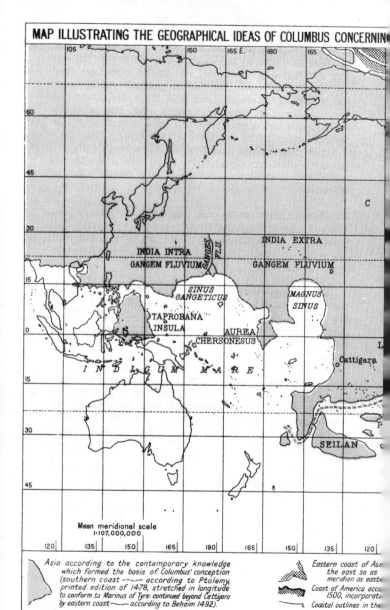

INDIA INTRA
GANGEM FLUVIUM

INDIA EXTRA
GANGEM FLUVIUM

GANGES FLU.

SINUS
GANGETICUS

MAGNUS
SINUS

TAPROBANA
INSULA

AUREA
CHERSONESUS

Cattigara

I N D I C U M   M A R E

SEILAN

Mean meridional scale
1:107,000,000

*Asia according to the contemporary knowledge
which formed the basis of Columbus' conception
(southern coast ----- according to Ptolemy,
printed edition of 1478, stretched in longitude
to conform to Marinus of Tyre; continued beyond Cattigara
by eastern coast ——— according to Behaim 1492).*

*Eastern coast of As
the east so as
meridian as easte*

*Coast of America acco
1500, incorporat*

*Coastal outlines in the*

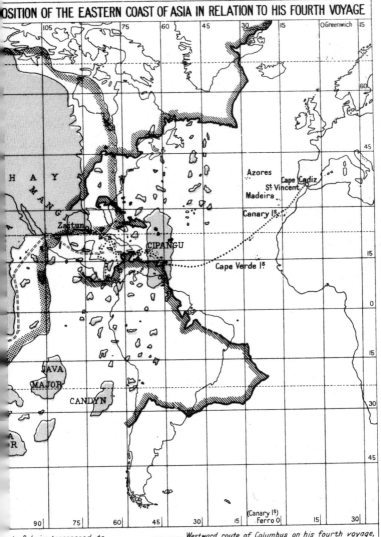

Azores
Cape Cadiz
St Vincent
Madeira
Canary Is.
Cape Verde Is.

H  A  Y
M A N G I
Zaitun
CIPANGU
JAVA
MAJOR
CANDYN

OGreenwich

(Canary Is)
Ferro O

to Behaim transposed to
e cape at Zaitun on same
ba, which Columbus took for Asia.
world map of Juan de la Cosa
eries up to that date.
tion according to modern maps.

.......... Westward route of Columbus on his fourth voyage,
1502-03.

======= Route Columbus believed he was following along the coast
of Asia on his fourth voyage and continuation he
had at one time considered following to reach India.

*Caravel off the Cape of Good Hope
(Atlas of Guillaume le Testu, 1556).*

world-map drawn by his own hand, one of those he mentions having executed?

Columbus could not hope to embark on his great adventure without the aid of a sovereign, and the position of his wife's family facilitated his being heard at the Court of Portugal. It was doubtless in the year 1484 that John II ordered his court scholars to examine Columbus' proposals. As to the nature of these proposals, the only record we have is an account (based on reliable sources, and written about the year 1539) by the Portuguese court historian, João de Barros:

> Columbus, an eloquent man, a good Latin scholar, but much puffed up with pride . . . having read Marco Polo, arrived at the conclusion that one could reach Cypango and other unknown lands via an ocean route;

the discovery of the Azores proved that there must be other lands lying even farther to the west. Full of the dreams that came to him from his continual travels and the conversations he had had with men of our land well-known for their past discoveries, he came to ask Dom João for ships to sail to Cypango through the Ocean Sea. . . . The King, seeing his stubbornness, sent him to Dom Diogo Ortiz, the bishop of Ceuta, to Master Rorigo and to Master Jozé, whose authority he customarily accepted in matters of geography and discovery, and they all considered Columbus' words to be vain, for all that he said was founded on imagination or on fictions such as the isle of Cypango of Marco Polo.

The Genoese was therefore dismissed, though not discourteously, for we gather in passing from one of his marginal notes that in 1485 he was present at court at the very moment that the King heard Master Jozé, his physician-cosmographer, report on observations of latitude taken on the Guinea coast.

Why had Columbus not won the confidence of John II? It is probable that the court cosmographers who questioned Columbus were not at all convinced by his assertions that the ocean was small, and his calculations of the size of a terrestrial degree no doubt seemed erroneous to them. (We can detect in Barros' account a note of condescension toward the self-schooled navigator.) Ferdinand tells us, moreover, that the King could not bear the thought of granting the honorary prerogatives – golden spurs and the title of Admiral – that Columbus demanded in the event of his success. But being raised to the nobility was quite the usual procedure in such cases, and the title of Admiral, we may recall, had been granted to a Genoese a century before. Perhaps the King found the thought of the cost of the enterprise less bearable still, for expenses would have had to be assumed by the Crown.

The truth is that John II preferred to concentrate all his navigators' efforts on another objective: finding a sea route around Africa and thus opening a new route to the Indies. The Portuguese were very close to realizing their aim: in 1482 Diogo Cão had sailed far beyond the equator and discovered the mouth of the Congo. The moment was not far off when Bartholomeu Dias would round the Cape of Good Hope in the year 1487.

This is not to say, however, that the King was not interested in ocean exploration. Recent Portuguese historians such as J. Cortesão even believe that there were people in Lisbon who already suspected – or were certain of – the existence of the continent of South America. The testimony of Columbus himself on this point still puzzles us: during his third voyage to the New World in 1498 he sailed very far south, to the latitude of Sierra Leone, before setting a course westward, "in order to verify," he writes, "what Dom João maintains: namely, that there lies toward the west a very large mainland." (Columbus did indeed find such a mainland, along the delta of the Orinoco.) · Antilia continued to haunt the imaginations of the islanders: in this very year – 1485 – when Columbus finally gave up seeking the patronage of the Court of Portugal, John II was negotiating with a certain Fernão Dulmo, who offered to outfit two caravels at his own expense to go in search of Antilia. This attempt was but another in a long series of expeditions that had sailed westward from the Azores, and had always failed in their mission. The Court of Lisbon had good reason to believe that the route to the Indies could be found more easily to the south than to the west.

Columbus left Portugal suddenly, probably in the summer of 1485; Ferdinand and Las Casas, his biographers, say that he departed "in secret." It was once thought that Columbus feared that the King, anxious to keep to himself the secret of the ocean routes to which Columbus had been privy during his long stay, would resent his departure. We are inclined today, however, to believe that he wished to avoid prosecution by certain of his creditors – a hypothesis apparently confirmed by several clauses in his will. His plans at this juncture are not immediately apparent. No doubt he envisaged several possibilities: he could betake himself either to the Court of Castile or the Court of France, and he doubtless was awaiting some providential circumstance. It was quite natural that he should head for Spain first, for it lay close by. He disembarked at Palos, a port on the Andalusian coast not far from Huelva where his wife's sister, who had married a Castilian, lived. Holding his little son Diego, who was then about five years old, by the hand, he stopped a league away at the Franciscan friary of La Rábida. There then occurred an episode such as might be found in a novel; this incident was later recounted by Fernández García, a physician from Palos. Despite the obscurities arising from the fact that the physician includes in his account incidents that occurred during one of Columbus' later visits to La Rábida, the facts can be reconstructed as follows: the stranger rang the bell at the gate and asked for a drink of water for little Diego, who was exhausted. The Prior, Fray Juan Pérez de Marchena (a Portuguese) welcomed him warmly, and found the stranger's conversation especially interesting, for from this coast sailed many expeditions to distant places. The Prior then introduced him to a friar who had a reputation as a "cosmographer": Fray Antonio de Marchena, guardian of the Franciscan province of Seville, who understood Columbus' plan and encouraged him. "This friar was the only person who came constantly to my aid," he was to write later. Little Diego remained at La Rábida, in the care of the friars.

From Palos Columbus next went to Seville, a great commercial metropolis where a large colony of Genoese had a whole quarter to themselves. There he established relations with the Florentine banker Berardi, who for many years was to lend him financial support. His new friends introduced him to a Spanish grandee, the Duke of Medina-Celi, an extremely wealthy man who owned a private merchant fleet and offered to outfit, at his own expense, the armada necessary for the enterprise. But Columbus wanted royal patronage, and made it known that he intended to go to the Court of France. The Duke thereupon sent him to the Queen.

"The Queen" was in this case Isabella of Castile, the wife of Ferdinand of Aragon; these two young sovereigns are referred to as "Los Reyes Católicos" – Their Catholic Majesties. The royal couple had been immediately confronted with both a civil war and a war against Portugal.

In 1479 a peace treaty had been concluded which settled, at least for the time being, the maritime rivalry existing between the two countries: Castile renounced all claims to the African coast and the Azores; Portugal recognized Spain's right to occupy the Canary Islands, lying in African waters farther to the south. Their Catholic Majesties now had their hands free to pursue their Grand Design: the expulsion of the Moors from Spain. When Columbus arrived in the sovereign states of Castile and Aragon, the death struggle against the Kingdom of Granada had already begun.

Columbus' first audience with the young sovereigns took place in May of 1486 in the city of Córdova, where they were temporarily holding court.

Isabella was thirty-five years old – the same age as the Genoese. The Queen's secretary, Fernando del Pulgar, writes:

> She was blonde, with blue-green eyes, a gracious mien, and a lovely, merry face; most dignified in her movements and countenance; a woman of great intelligence and great wisdom.

We may add that she was by nature passionate, profoundly Christian, and highly conscious of the duties imposed upon her by her faith and rank.

Ferdinand was a year younger:

> Well-proportioned, ... a fine horseman, incomparably skilled at jousting; master of himself in all things, for neither anger nor pleasure produced any change in him. ...

He was also a consummate diplomat, whom Machiavelli came to admire greatly. Moreover, he was a sincere Christian.

Regarding this first interview, we have only Las Casas' few brief lines:

> Their Majesties took note of his request, received it with gracious countenance, and decided to submit the matter to a commission of learned men ... for at the moment they were much concerned with the war.

48

*Celestial Jerusalem.*
*(From the Apocalypse of Angers, a fifteenth century tapestry).*

No clear decision had been made; far from it. But Columbus – "tall in stature, with an aquiline nose, and hair prematurely white," as his son Ferdinand describes him – must have impressed them favorably. From the beginning his grave demeanor, his passionate eloquence when he spoke of the mission that God had bid him fulfill, moved the Queen to confidence and sympathy. "Everyone made mock of my project. Your Majesty alone gave proof of faith and loyalty, inspired, surely, by the light of the Holy Spirit," Columbus later wrote.

From this time on, the Genoese received a small pension from the Court, and took up residence in Córdova, where he consorted with fellow countrymen whom he met in a shop kept by a Genoese physician-apothecary, the favorite rendezvous of those interested in "physics" and "astrology." There he met a certain Pedro de Harana, a Basque, who introduced him to his sister, Beatriz Enríquez. Columbus, who was now a man well into his thirties, took the young twenty-year-old girl as his mistress. This liaison did not end in marriage, to the great chagrin of those modern admirers of Columbus who hoped to see him canonized. In 1488 a son was born of this union, Ferdinand, who became a man of learning and an eminent humanist. Though Columbus continued to aid Beatriz financially, he later gave up living with her, doubtless at the time that he entered the Third Order of Saint Francis. (He may even have taken a vow of chastity, for we do not find him implicated in scandals involving women during his years in the Indies, where morals were extremely lax.) Several close relatives of Beatriz joined Columbus in his great enterprise: her cousin commanded the fleet on the first voyage, and her brother a caravel on the third. In his will Columbus betrays deep remorse in regard to Beatriz, "a person who much weigheth on my conscience. It would not be seemly to write herein the reason thereof."

At the end of 1486 Columbus followed the Court to its new residence in Salamanca. There he made the acquaintance of the Dominican Father Diego de Deza, a professor of theology at the College of San Estéban, and later the preceptor of the Infante and a bishop. In him Columbus found an intelligent defender: "There were but two churchmen ever loyal to me" – Father Marchena and Father Deza, a Franciscan and a Dominican. (Let us note Columbus' ability to make faithful friends; we shall find that there were others, Italians and Spaniards, who gave him their constant esteem and support. This could hardly be the case if the Genoese were the unscrupulous braggart he is often made out to be.)

Taking advantage of their stay in the university town of Salamanca, the sovereigns assembled a commission of learned men and scholars and ordered it to examine Columbus' project. Dr. Rodrigo Maldonado, a City Counselor, later wrote:

I was among those who held audience with the Admiral in regard to his project. All of them declared it impossible, but he defiantly insisted that it was possible. The sovereigns consequently postponed their answer, though they did not take from him all hope that they would consider the matter when they were less occupied.

Columbus' persistence was not rewarded until 1492. He later wrote:

I endured six or seven years of great tribulation, explaining as best I could how great a service could be done Our Lord by bringing His Holy Name and Faith to so many nations, to the honor and glory of these great Sovereigns. I showed them the writings of reliable scholars telling of the great riches of those lands; I had also to invoke the opinion of cosmographers. . . . All those who had heard me out thought my enterprise a jest. But despite the travail that I endured, I was certain that all would one day come to be, for in truth "all things shall pass away, but the Word of the Lord God shall not pass away." So saith Our Lord, Who spoke so clearly of these lands through the mouth of Isaiah in so many passages of Holy Scripture, and said that it was from Spain that the Glad Tidings of His Holy Name would spread.

During his long wait, as the war with Granada dragged on and no decision regarding his project was handed down, Columbus renewed his negotiations with the Court of Portugal in 1488. John II sent the following reply:

To our most special friend Columbus: we have seen the letter that you wrote us. We desire greatly to see you . . . and send you our safe-conduct so that you may have naught to fear from our judicial authorities.

(It is probable that Columbus feared that he would be prosecuted by his creditors.) King John at this point had had no news from Bartholomeu Dias, who had set out to sail around Africa, and Dulmo's voyage westward had been a miserable failure. This explains the King's renewed interest in Columbus.

*Granada: fortifications of the Alhambra*

Columbus spent several months in Lisbon, where he rejoined his brother. But at this juncture Bartholomeu Dias suddenly returned with an unexpected piece of news: "He announced to the King that he had sailed as far as the Cape of Good Hope, and showed him a chart of the voyage. I was present at court that day," Columbus wrote in a note in his *Imago mundi*. Now that a route to the Indies to the south and east was open to him, John II had no further reason to keep Columbus at court. It was doubtless at this point that the two brothers made plans to present the project to the King of England. We know (through Ferdinand's account) that Bartholomew went to the Court of England and showed Henry VII a chart on which were marked the lands "that he and his brother intended to discover,"

53

together with Latin verses invoking the authority of Ptolemy and Pliny.

Christopher returned to Spain. The end of 1489 found him in the royal camp outside the Moorish stronghold of Baza. Two Franciscan friars now sought audience with Their Catholic Majesties, for they bore an ultimatum from the Sultan of Egypt: unless the Sovereigns of Castile abandoned the war against Granada, the Sultan would raze the Holy City of Jerusalem. It is possible that Columbus was present at this audience; in any case he knew what it had been about. His constant preoccupation with Jerusalem, which was to haunt him till his death, began perhaps at this very moment. On finding his first gold mine in the "Indies," he noted in his journal:

> Three years hence, Your Majesties may make ready to go forth to reconquer Jerusalem, for I have always proposed that all the profit from my enterprise be used for the reconquest of Jerusalem.

These years of inactivity gave Columbus time to complete his plans. He drew up several charts and world-maps – among them one he showed the sovereigns several times "in order to inspire in them the desire to know these lands," as his future friend, the chronicler Andrés Bernáldez writes. (In the Paris National Library is a chart which we are certain belongs to this period between 1488 and 1492, and which Charles de la Roncière believed there was reason to ascribe to Columbus. It is a portulan-atlas of Europe and North Africa, with a small world-map attached to it; the explanatory legends on both charts bear a striking resemblance to annotations made by Columbus in his copy of the *Imago mundi*. But the absence of any indication of Cypango and the location of Antilia far to the north prove either that the chart is not his or that he was attempting to keep his ideas to himself.)

He now bought a printed Latin edition of the *Book of Ser Marco Polo*. He also came by the Latin translation of the *Book of Travels* ascribed to Sir John Mandeville, which first appeared in 1484. The author of this book had supposedly traveled to the heart of

China in the fourteenth century, and had worked into his account material not only from Marco Polo but from accounts of other travelers as well – among them an account by Piano Carpini, a Papal Ambassador to Tartary, interspersed with legendary tales of animals and men from medieval bestiaries. A passage such as the following must have set the future discoverer to dreaming:

> A brave man once set out, long ago, to circle the earth. And so it was that he passed through India and Ultra-India, and five thousand leagues beyond, and after many a season went around the whole world. . . . He said that he had seen the full circle of the heavens, and had come back around to his own country.

We are so accustomed today to the idea of "going around the world" that it is difficult for us to appreciate the mentality of medieval man. Since proof was to be found in Aristotle, the fact that the earth is round was, of course, no longer a matter for discussion. But how many mysteries still remained! There was above all the famous question of the Antipodes: were there, people wondered, dry lands in the hemisphere opposite theirs, either in the southern hemisphere or the western? And if such lands existed, were they inhabited? On the first point opinions differed, for some people, following the view of the ancients, believed that the ocean occupied most of the globe. On the second point Saint Augustine had given a clear answer in the negative: the first reason being that – as Lactantius had pointed out – it was difficult to imagine that there were men who walked about head downward; and the main reason being that it would be contrary to the divine scheme of things if there were men who could not be reached by the Gospel because they were cut off by the ocean or by a torrid zone, both of which were thought to be impossible to cross.

This opinion, which had been upheld by Nicholas of Lyra in the fourteenth century, prevailed in Castile. But Albertus Magnus on the other hand – and the Thomist school as a general rule – argued that it was not impossible – but merely difficult – to cross the torrid zone. The facts were beginning to confirm this view, and on the margin of his *Imago mundi* Columbus noted: "In our day the Portuguese navigate in these [torrid] regions; they have many inhabitants, and below the equator there has been constructed the fortress of Mina, which I have seen." There were no difficulties, then, so far as the Southern Antipodes were concerned. But Columbus was anxious to reveal to the world the "Western Antipodes" – this was the name that the humanist Peter Martyr would later use to hail Columbus' discovery when news of it reached Spain. In his *History of Venice* another contemporary, Pietro Bembo, gives this summary of the project proposed by Columbus to Ferdinand and Isabella:

> [Columbus claimed] that it was naught but a vain fiction of the ancients to believe that no more than two parts of the world were habitable: for it would be absurd for God to have created the world and have left the greater part of it useless, as it would be were it to contain no men; [he also claimed] that that which writers refer to as the ocean is not a vast empty expanse, but rather is filled with islands and inhabited lands; that the globe, along its whole circumference, shares in the vital *aura*.

Describing his great project after the fact, Columbus employs these lofty terms:

> I took upon myself the mission of messenger, announcing to these sovereigns the new heaven and the new earth of which Our Lord speaks in the *Apocalypse* through the mouth of Saint John, as before he had spoken through the mouth of Isaiah.

Columbus indeed envisaged a "new earth," a "new world" (the expression is his) – "new" in the sense of not yet having been reached by the Glad Tidings of the Gospel. There is obviously a certain confusion here of two planes, two orders of reality: the geographic and the supernatural. But for a Christian of the Middle Ages supernatural realities were not alien to our terrestrial

*The earliest portrait of Columbus.*
*(Galleria Gioviana, Como).*

globe, which was taken to be the very center of the created universe: was not the Terrestrial Paradise located in a certain mountainous region of the Orient, and Hell in the bowels of the earth? And scientific curiosity – as we would call it – was motivated largely by a Christian imperative: to bring within the orbit of the Church a still unknown half of the world was to obey to the letter the charge of Our Lord to spread the Gospel to the ends of the earth. The world must be brought to its appointed end, united in one Christian kingdom. Discovery and

57

religious perspectives are inseparable. Columbus sincerely believed that God Himself had inspired his mission to the Indies, that if Queen Isabella understood the grand scope of his plan, "it was through the light of the Holy Spirit."

Since the Western Antipodes lay – by hypothesis – in the region of the Indies, Columbus believed that he would find there the kingdom of the Grand Khan, and believed that bringing this potentate the friendship of Christians and the light of faith was a highly praiseworthy endeavor. He had good reason to suppose that he would be warmly welcomed. Had not Marco Polo reported that in 1266 his father and his uncle, who were then in Peking, were sent back to Rome by Kublai Khan, the reigning Emperor (whose mother was a Nestorian Christian), to beg the Pope to send him "as many as one hundred wise men to teach the Christian doctrine"? At the time of his negotiations with the Court of Castile, Columbus recalls this fact: "The Grand Khan and his predecessors have on many occasions sent ambassadors to Rome to ask for learned men to teach our Holy Faith, but the Holy Father has never sent them." And when he at last set sail for the Indies, he carried with him a letter of credence from Ferdinand and Isabella to the Grand Khan. The affable disposition of this potentate and his subjects was an encouraging note that Columbus had come across – in a passage in the *Historia rerum* of Aeneas Silvius in particular: "The populace of Cathay is most docile; this is a country which lies at the beginning of the Indies, just opposite Spain."

Summing up his years of waiting, Columbus later wrote: "As it was also necessary that I speak of the temporal aspect of the enterprise, I showed the sovereigns the writings of reliable scholars telling of the great riches of those lands." These writings were no doubt the *Historia rerum*, which spoke of the abundance of gold and pearls that lay hidden in Cathay, and the *Imago mundi*, which described the islands of the Indian Ocean as being full of precious stones and pearls. He was probably also referring to Biblical commentaries – of the *Book of Kings* and of *Chronicles* – which spoke of the fabulous treasures of Tharsis and Ophir, to which King

Solomon sent a fleet to look for gold, ivory, monkeys, and precious woods. Because they doubtless seemed to him altogether too sketchy, Columbus made copious annotations of those passages of the *Imago mundi* that mentioned these mysterious kingdoms. And he was later to write an encomium of gold that has scandalized his modern critics: "Gold is an excellent thing. When one possesses it, one can do as he pleaseth in this world – even bring souls to Paradise." But for Columbus gold was, more than any other thing, the means to accomplish works of faith. Again and again he insisted that the entire profits from his discovery be used for religious ends. Just as the gold of Ophir enabled Solomon to furnish the Temple with magnificent liturgical adorn- ments, so gold recalled to Columbus the mystic the idea of Jerusalem: the deliverance of the Holy Sepulchre, the complement of his great dream of circumnavigating the globe.

This air of a great crusade took on special overtones in Spain. Ferdinand and Isabella's fight to the death against the enemies within their borders – the Judaizers – and their enemies without – the Moslems – seemed to be the realization of a providential plan, and opened up vast perspectives. Revived by the Aquitanian monk Jean de Roquetaillade, there had circulated for a century a number of prophecies attributed to the legendary Merlin the Magician and to Saint Joachim of Flores, the twelfth- century anchorite saint who had predicted the disappear- ance of the sect of Mohammed and a Christian renais- sance. A king was awaited, a "son of the eagle" who would "subjugate the Moors of Granada," then "recover the Holy Land." With Ferdinand's accession to the throne, these prophecies seemed on the point of being fulfilled.[1] These were signs that Columbus eagerly scrutinized. How many times he later wrote: "Abbot Joachim says that he who is to rebuild the House of Zion will come from Spain!"

These grandiose dreams gave Columbus the patience to wait out this time as best he could. Though these

---

[1] See the curious document entitled "Souhaits de bienvenue à Ferdinand le Catholique" in *Romania* XI (1933), p. 333 ff.

were difficult years, he did succeed in making contacts in influential circles. The Cardinal of Spain, Mendoza, whom people called the "Third Sovereign," held him in great esteem, having noticed that this foreigner "was wise, a fine conversationalist, and a sound thinker" – as Oviedo, the Royal Chronicler, put it. The great financier Luis de Santangel – who doubtless had Jewish antecedents – and his relative Gabriel Sánchez, the former Keeper of the Privy Purse and later the Royal Treasurer of Aragon, likewise esteemed him, and were to have occasion to prove it. The Papal Legate, Alessandro Geraldini, a Genoese, aided his compatriot to the best of his ability and became a loyal friend.

Columbus' situation was nonetheless precarious, both materially and psychologically. He had again taken to drawing and selling charts. And the sarcasm heaped on his great dream, whose fulfillment seemed ever farther away, was hard to bear.

After his stay in England, Bartholomew Columbus was now in France at the court of Charles VIII. Might the King of France not be the man chosen of God to realize the great enterprise? (There were certain commentators who saw in Charles VIII the man who would fulfill the prophecy of Joachim of Flores.) Had promises been made Columbus by the English and the French? We have no proof, except what he himself says (in a letter to Ferdinand in May, 1505): "I received letters from the Kings of England and of France, which the Queen [Isabella] saw and read, and communicated to her Royal Council."

Be this as it may, Columbus by 1491 was about to lose patience and leave Spain. He went off to Palos, and from there to the monastery of La Rábida, doubtless to see his son Diego once again. And once more his destiny was suddenly changed. His friend the Prior, Fray Juan Pérez, on finding him completely discouraged, took matters into his own hands and summoned from Palos García Fernández, a physician "versed in astrology." Dr. Fernández later wrote (at the time of the litigation between the Crown and Columbus' heirs):

I came forthwith. All three of us began to discuss

the matter. Following this conversation, we sent a messenger to Queen Isabella with a letter from the aforementioned Juan Pérez, who had been her confessor. Fourteen days later, the Queen wrote to the aforementioned friar, thanking him for his intervention and ordering him to come to her at court.

Since the month of July, 1491, the sovereigns had been holding court in Santa-Fé, a camp laid out like a city a few kilometers from the beleaguered city of Granada. Immediately following the arrival of the Franciscan friar, Isabella sent for Columbus, forwarding him enough money to provide himself with a mule.

Thus it was that he found himself – at the age of forty – within reach of his goal. The commission of scholars and theologians was again convoked. Certain of them, taking up the arguments of Saint Augustine, objected that it was impossible to sail as far as the Antipodes. Geraldini (from whose account we know of this session) then appealed to the wisdom of Mendoza, and had no difficulty in convincing him that the Portuguese had proved, several decades before, that navigation in the torrid zone was possible. The final decision fell to the Royal Council. Columbus again showed his world-map to the sovereigns, maintaining that the islands and mainland of the Indies lay only a short sail away. They were impressed by his conviction: "What you announced to us came to pass as if you had seen it before speaking of it to us," the sovereigns were to write him just after his discovery.

Several more months passed, then Granada, the last stronghold of the Moors, finally capitulated. Columbus took part in the royal procession which entered the reconquered city on January 2, 1492: "On that day I saw the royal standards raised on the towers of the Alhambra, and saw the King of the Moors come out through the gates of the city and kiss the hands of Your Majesties."

As far as finances were concerned, Columbus' demands were moderate: two million *maravedis* to outfit three caravels. Even this, however, would be a great burden on the Royal Treasury, which was completely empty. As for the prerogatives that Columbus demanded in the

61

event that his voyage was successful, they seemed exorbitant: the title of Admiral of the Ocean Sea, and all admiralty jurisdiction pertaining thereunto – making him the equal of the King's uncle, the Admiral of Castile; the offices of Viceroy and Governor of all islands and mainlands discovered; and the power to appoint and remove all officials, this power to be transmissible to his descendants. (Had the sovereigns been able to foresee the extent of the lands opened up by Columbus, they would have been more reluctant still!) This lofty attitude is quite consistent with Columbus' messianic character; this was the man who later wrote, with towering pride:

> Humility showed me the little that I counted for, but knowing the great message that I bore, I felt myself the equal of both Crowns [i.e., of Castile and Aragon].

He was summarily dismissed by the sovereigns. But as he rode away, a Captain of the Guards dispatched by the Queen overtook him two leagues from Granada and ordered him to turn back. What had happened? Ferdinand Columbus writes that Isabella's sudden change of mind was due to the intervention of Santangel, who reproached her for abandoning a "magnanimous" enterprise in the service of God, and offered to advance her the necessary funds. There must also have been pressure from the bishop Diego de Deza, now preceptor of the Infante, for Columbus writes: "His Eminence the Bishop was the cause of my remaining in Castile, for I was already on my way out of the country."

To bring the Reconquest to a triumphant conclusion, Ferdinand and Isabella still had to settle the matter of the Jews. On March 31, 1492, the sovereigns' edict expelling all Jews in the peninsula was proclaimed in Santa-Fé. This was an odious measure, but one which Columbus doubtless approved, for the Jews were held responsible for the "Judaic" heresy that had spread throughout the peninsula among supposed Christian converts; Columbus later praised the sovereigns for "having destroyed those not willing to confess the Father, Son, and Holy Ghost," i.e., these *conversos*. As for

Columbus, his enterprise, and indeed his every act, was done in the name of the Holy Trinity.

The *Capitulations,* as the agreement between the Navigator and Their Catholic Majesties is called, were signed on April 17. Columbus was to receive, if he succeeded, the title of Admiral and the viceroyalty and governorship of all "islands and *terra firma*" discovered; he was to have the right to one-tenth of the gold, pearls, spices, and any other products of value that might be discovered; he was to contribute one-eighth of the expenses of the undertaking, and would receive one-eighth of the profits. In solemn confirmation of these provisions, as set forth in letters patent dated Granada, April 30, Their Catholic Majesties specified that the titles of Admiral and Viceroy were to be granted to his descendants in perpetuity. It was stipulated that the Genoese, who was to be raised to the nobility, would henceforth be called Don Cristóbal *Colón.* Why this change of spelling? "He refashioned his name," Ferdinand tells us, "in order to make it conform to the custom in his new country," and adds that he did so for the further reason that *Colón* evokes the idea of *colonizing,* winning souls for God. It is surprising that the future Christ-Bearer did not instead take advantage of the symbolic possibilities of *columba,* the dove of the Holy Spirit. (Ferdinand develops this image in the manner it deserves, and future "hagiographers" of Columbus such as Léon Bloy and Paul Claudel use it to magnificent effect.) It is not beyond the realm of possibility that this Genoese commoner also wanted to suggest that he was related to Admiral Coullon, who was called *Colón* in Spain. "I am not the first Admiral in my family," he was one day to write, a sentence whose meaning is still a mystery.

The funds needed to outfit the three caravels Columbus had asked for were raised without difficulty. Santangel advanced the Crown one million *maravedis,* and Columbus furnished the other million, thanks to loans made him by Genoese compatriots and the banker Berardi. Before leaving the Court, Columbus had letters of credence in Latin made out to him, in blank and in triplicate, to be presented to the Grand Khan or any other potentate of the Indies. This fact alone would suffice to prove that Columbus' real destination was the Indies, despite the opinion of such hypercritical authorities as Harrisse and Vignaud, who maintain that his only objective was certain islands of the Ocean Sea.

These same historians, whom Columbus' most recent critics have followed, have also attempted to detract from the merits of the Genoese by attributing a prime role to a certain Martín Alonso Pinzón during the months that preceded the embarkation. The controversy between the "pro-Pinzón" and "pro-Columbus" factions began, in fact, shortly after the death of Columbus: the descendants of Martín Pinzón sought at that time to prove that Columbus had been no more than the nominal head of an enterprise that had gotten under way through Martín's efforts. This statement was made during a lawsuit instigated by the Spanish Crown in an attempt to annul the hereditary privileges of Columbus' descendants. Survivors of the expedition and residents of Palos were consequently interrogated; the records of their testimony are lively documents, and a valuable aid in the reconstruction of this period of Columbus' life.

Martín Pinzón was a wealthy shipowner who outfitted both privateers and merchants vessels; he was also an expert navigator, for he had participated in the maritime wars with Portugal and sailed along the coasts of Guinea. Being something of a "cosmographer," Martín – like many another navigator – was anxious to discover new lands. Martín's son later recounted, during the litigation between the Crown and the heirs of Columbus, the following curious story concerning his father, who had gone to Rome in 1491:

> One day when he was in the library of the Pope, where he frequently went to see a member of the Pope's court who was a great cosmographer and had numerous manuscripts at his disposal, he began to speak with him of lands that had not yet been discovered, and told him on several occasions that he wished to outfit two vessels to go in search of them.

The librarian then allegedly presented him with a

document describing a voyage made by the Queen of Sheba, first to Spain, then from Spain to Cypango, "via an easy route that must be followed as far as 95° west longitude." On his return to Palos Pinzón presumably passed this document on to Colombus and thus revived the latter's courage to renew his negotiations with the Court.

This story is not impossible – although there is no

*"I set my course..." Allegorical drawing, early sixteenth century.*
*(Palazzo Ducale, Genoa).*

mention of this fabled voyage in any literary account that has come down to us. It is certain in any event that Pinzón was interested in the search for Cypango, as is evident from the account in the journal that Columbus kept during their voyage together. The meeting of these two men possessed of the same great dream was thus a fortunate coincidence. Would Martín Pinzón have outfitted two caravels and sailed toward the mysterious west even if he had not met the Genoese? Would he have discovered the Antilles? We will never know. . . .

Columbus returned to the port of Palos in the month of May, 1492, armed with a royal ordinance: the citizens of Palos, who the year before had been the object of a collective punishment for privateering, were required to furnish two caravels and their crews for "our Captain, Cristóbal Colón." The inhabitants of Palos were hardy mariners, certainly, but sailing off with this stranger into vast unexplored expanses of ocean terrified them. "They all thought that he and anyone who would sail with him were marked for death," one of the witnesses testified during the lawsuit.

Things changed when Martín Pinzón decided to participate in the great voyage. Another witness gave this testimony: "If Martín Alonso had not given two ships to the Admiral, he could not have gone through with his expedition, for no one knew him and he would not have found men to go with him."

The two ships referred to were the caravels *Pinta* and *Niña,* one of which was to be commanded by Martín and the other by his brother Vicente. The third vessel, the *Santa María,* was a *nao* – a heavier ship than a caravel – chartered by Columbus from its owner, Juan de la Cosa. (It was originallly called *La Gallega* – the Galician – but Columbus insisted on placing it beneath the guardianship of the Blessed Virgin.) The most difficult task was signing on a crew. According to one of the witnesses at the trial, Pinzón called a meeting and addressed the men in these words: "Come on, friends! Sail with us on this voyage. You will find houses with roofs of gold [as in Marco Polo's account] and win fame and fortune." Pinzón then read them his famous document.

The timid were not the only ones; there were also the skeptical, who said: "Many Portuguese have sailed off to explore the ocean to the west, but they have never found anything." But the plot now thickens, comes more and more to resemble a novel. An old pilot named Pedro Vásquez de la Frontera came upon the scene, telling anyone willing to listen to him that long before, in the year 1452, he had sailed with the Portuguese navigator Diogo de Teive on a voyage into the Atlantic in search of the Indies; they had sailed beyond the Azores to the southwest, and had encountered beds of grass [the Sargasso Sea] that had halted them; they then had sailed northeast, hoping to reach the island of Brazil, and had discovered during their voyage the island of Flores (the most westerly of the islands in the Azores archipelago); the winds had borne them northward as far as the latitude of Ireland; they had then turned back. The pilot was convinced that lands would be found, if the wind were favorable, by setting a course *due west*. An inhabitant of Palos reported:

> This Pedro Vásquez counseled Columbus and Martín Alonso Pinzón, and urged the men on, telling them publicly that they should all ship on this voyage, for they would discover a rich land; he went about saying this in the public squares.

About a hundred men were finally signed on. The majority of the able seamen were Andalusians. There was also a highly undisciplined Basque clique, which centered about Juan de la Cosa. Also aboard were several royal functionaries: an Arabic, Greek, and Hebrew interpreter of Jewish origin named Luis de Torres (it was evidently hoped that the Grand Khan would have some notion of these languages!); a Marshal of the Fleet, Diego de Harana, the cousin of Beatriz Enríquez; a Fleet Secretary, Rodrigo de Escobedo; a Royal Commissioner, charged with seeing that the Crown got its share of the revenues. Each ship had a surgeon. Also aboard were artisans: the caulkers and coopers necessary for the proper maintenance of the vessels.

There were no men-at-arms aboard, though "lombards" – cannons – were carried. Nor were there any priests. Columbus did not intend to establish colonies in the Indies on this voyage. He preferred, rather, to explore as far afield as possible, and was carrying enough supplies for a whole year. (The need to prosyletize became apparent to him, however, from the moment that he came in contact with the natives.) In cases of mortal danger, if no priest were at hand, the Church allowed – and recommended – mutual confession.

They sailed on August 3. As was the custom, all hands confessed their sins and took communion. Just before sunrise the three ships, with unfurled sails on which huge crosses were painted, sailed down the river Tinto, then down the river Odiel toward the sea, rounding the promontory on whose heights stood the monastery of La Rábida. The heavy *Santa María*, of one hundred tons' burthen, was the flagship and took the lead, followed by the graceful *Niña* and *Pinta*. Several attempts have been made to reconstruct the three glorious caravels (only two of which really deserve to be called caravels), though Morison affirms that we do not have sufficient data to construct accurate replicas. It is interesting, nonetheless, to see the *Santa María III*, constructed in 1929 by Julio Guillén, director of the Madrid Naval Museum, for it allows us to imagine to kind of life the Captain-General and his men led. They lived in extremely close quarters: the entire crew slept on the deck. Only Columbus and the "Master" – or First Officer – had cabins in the forecastle. The monotonous shipboard life took its rhythm from the chanteys that accompanied the daily tasks on board ship, and from the prayers for which the crew was assembled several times a day. Columbus brought with him a breviary, which he had doubtless learned to use at La Rábida. The lyric height his style often reaches has a distinctly Biblical accent. This lyricism becomes particularly intense when he is at sea, for this is his real element. On his copy of Ptolemy's *Geography* he wrote these splendid verses: "Mirabiles elationes maris. Mirabilis Dominus in altis." [Wondrous are the tumultuous swells of the sea. Wondrous is God in the ocean depths.]

The Captain-General immediately began to keep a log to be sent to the King and Queen of Castile. In the Prologue he writes:

I set sail on Friday, August 3, and set a course for the Canary Islands belonging to Your Majesties, in order that I might thence set my course and sail on till I should reach the Indies and fulfill the mission to princes of that land that was given unto me by Your Majesties, and thus execute that which they would have me do. To this purpose, I have resolved to note every detail of this voyage most carefully, writing down each night the events that the day has brought, and each day the events of the night previous. I moreover propose to make a new marine chart, upon which I shall set down the location of all the lands of the Ocean Sea, under their bearings by the compass rose; I shall furthermore set the whole down in a book, depicting it by latitude from the equator and by longitude west. [This latter promise was not kept, for lack of sufficient technical knowledge.] To accomplish my purpose, it will be necessary that I forgo sleep.

It would be fascinating to follow this account hour by hour, for it is not the usual ship's log giving only the course and the distance made good, but rather it is full of scientific, geographic, and religious descriptions and conclusions. The original manuscript of this precious document has disappeared, but Ferdinand Columbus and Las Casas had it in their possession. Las Casas published an edition of it, copying some passages of the original in their entirety, and summarizing others; he also used it in several chapters of his *History of the Indies*. We shall here confine ourselves to those episodes that are most noteworthy and best reveal the psychology of Columbus.

*Columbus' caravel and the islands of the "Indies."*
*(Woodcut, Basel, 1494, incunabulum preserved in the Bibliothèque Nationale, Paris)*

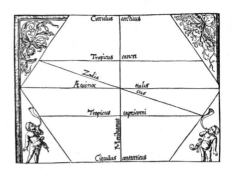

# THE NEW WORLD

Columbus headed directly for the Canaries, a possession of the Crown of Castile, "in order that I might thence set my course," as he writes in the Prologue of his journal. He indeed appears to have had a definite course in mind: the twenty-eighth parallel of north latitude, which he was to follow consistently. "Whatever the source of this opinion may have been, he affirmed that by setting a course straight west from Ferro Island [the most westerly of the Canary Islands] and sailing for a distance of about 750 leagues, one would find land." [Las Casas: *History of the Indies*, I, ch. 39.] Columbus apparently had on board a chart on which – as on the globe that Behaim was in the midst of constructing – the Canaries lay on the same parallel of latitude as the isle of Cypango (which in turn had a whole string of islands lying round about it). Furthermore, as Morison, an expert who has personally navigated sailing vessels, explains: "It has always been the plan of simple dead-reckoning navigators to get on the presumed latitudes of their destination, and run their easting or westing down until they reach it." [1] During his voyages along

---

[1]   Morison, *ibid.*, p. 157.

the coast of Africa the Genoese had moreover had the opportunity of observing that the Canaries lay in a zone of northeast tradewinds, and thus knew the advantages of this archipelago over that of the Azores, which lay farther north and was situated in a zone of westerlies – which accounts for the failure of the voyages attempted by the Portuguese. In Columbus' case, we must also add a chance factor: he benefited from the fact that this is the best season for sailing in these zones of the Atlantic, and was driven by the tradewinds to the fortieth meridian.

Reaching the Canaries on August 12, Columbus was detained at Las Palmas while damage incurred by the *Pinta* was repaired, then set sail for Gomera and anchored in the roadstead off the little town of San Sebastian. The lavish hospitality of her imposing castle was offered him by Beatriz de Peraza y Bobadilla, the young and beautiful widow of the Governor of the Canaries. The Captain-General was not indifferent to her charms, if we may believe Michele de Cuneo, a Genoese friend of Columbus' who saw them together on another occasion. They talked with those soon to be left behind, and Columbus wrote in his journal: "Many trustworthy Spaniards, natives of Ferro Island, swear that each year they see an island to the west."

On September 6, mass was said in the Church of the Assumption, and the three ships set sail. "On the 8th of September, at eight o'clock in the morning, a northeast wind came up and I set a course to the west," he writes. From this date on, Columbus each day noted in his log the distance they had made good, "but I decided to mark less than the actual distance made in order that my men should not be frightened if the voyage proved a long one." The same tactics were employed by the first officer and the captains of the other two caravels.

For ten days there was smooth sailing: the weather was splendid and the tradewinds steady. On September 17, "they found the seawater less salty, the air more and more balmy. All the sailors were in high spirits, and the ships vied with each other to see which would sight land first." On September 18, the *Pinta* took the lead, for "Martín Pinzón had seen a great flock of birds flying westward and hoped for a landfall that night." On the 19th Columbus totted up his dead reckoning and concluded that he had made four hundred leagues; he believed he was sailing "among islands, but these will be explored on the homeward passage, my plan being to push on to the Indies." [Columbus' journal.] There was a moment of panic when the pilots discovered that instead of pointing true north the compass needle varied a full point to the northwest (the first known report of the phenomenon of "magnetic variation"); but Columbus managed to calm the men by taking a sight on the North Star at dawn, an hour when there is practically no deviation.

They now entered the Sargasso Sea, and the surface of the ocean was transformed into one great floating meadow. Columbus and Pinzón had fortunately been warned of this phenomenon by Vásquez de la Frontera and knew that they needed only to sail through it to the other side.

Contrary winds now began to blow. "My men were quite delighted by this," Columbus wrote, for they were beginning to fear that they would have no wind for the return voyage. The wind then dropped, "and a heavy sea rose up, though there was no wind, which astonished everyone; . . . this rough sea was most useful to me; it was a sign such as had not appeared save in the time of the Jews, when they went out of Egypt, following Moses as he led them out of captivity." There were murmurs against the foreigner, "but because of the prodigious signs of God's favor given unto him, they held back from laying a hand on him," we read in Ferdinand's *History*.

Martín Pinzón now borrowed from the Captain-General a chart "on which were depicted certain islands," and concluded, on September 25, that they must be in the vicinity of those islands. That same day, he believed that he had sighted land; unfortunately, it was only a mirage. The crew began to grow restive: they had now been three weeks with no sight of land. The inactivity and the close quarters contributed to their dangerously touchy mood, which now turned against the man responsible for this voyage into the unknown. The murmurs took on a threatening note. "But with gracious and cheerful countenance, he raised their spirits; they would soon realize, he said, that he had told the truth." [Las Casas.]

On October 3, Columbus notes in his journal that he has probably overrun the islands marked on his chart, but that he "does not care to delay matters by beating to windward, for his object was to reach the Indies." On October 6, Pinzón, fearing that they had missed Cypango, demanded that they alter their course to the southwest; they had, indeed, gone far beyond the 750 leagues they had counted on. On October 7, Columbus ordered the course altered to the southwest, for he had seen flocks of migratory birds flying overhead in this direction. He ordered the ships to stay close to the *Santa María* at sunrise and sunset, "for these two hours are most favoable for seeing far in the distance." [Columbus' journal.] On October 10: "The crew could bear no more, and complained of the length of the voyage. Columbus cheered them as best he could, holding out to them the great hope of the profits they would have." The crew's disaffection now bordered on mutiny, especially aboard the flagship, where a clique of Basques and Galicians grouped about the First Officer, Juan de la Cosa, had proved to be troublemakers. Open mutiny did not break out, however. Columbus treats this subject with cautious reserve in his journal, but we have some inkling of the crew's state of mind from the depositions made by two old seamen during the litigation in 1512. According to the testimony of Pedro de Bilbao: "Several pilots and sailors wanted to turn back. The Admiral asked them to wait two or three days and within that time land would be sighted." Another witness: "I heard the sailors say that they were lost." During this famous trial witnesses for the Crown and Pinzón's heirs claimed that it was only because of Martín Pinzón that Columbus did not turn back. Accounts of the witnesses in this regard are contradictory. One of them says that the captain of the *Pinta* urged the Genoese to take strong measures: "String up a half-dozen of 'em." Others allege, on the contrary, that the Admiral was the only one who would not admit defeat. Francisco Morales testifies: "Juan

Niño later told me that the First Officers of the three ships wanted to return to Spain and formally requested the Admiral to do so. . . . He asked them to be patient yet three or four days more." Oviedo, the Royal Chronicler, who can hardly be suspected of partiality toward Columbus, gives a similar account: "Columbus raised the spirits of the downcast, especially the three brother captains and they agreed to sail on for three days more."

On October 11, there were many unmistakable signs of land: the branch of a tree in flower, a piece of carved wood, a plank, etc. When the entire crew of the *Santa María* was assembled at nightfall for the singing of the *Salve Regina*, the Captain-General enjoined the men to keep a good watch on the forecastle and a sharp lookout for land. At 10 p.m., an hour before moonrise, Columbus, on watch in the stern, saw a light, "but it was so uncertain a thing that he dared not call out that he had sighted land," and mentioned it to only two persons. Shortly thereafter, a seaman also saw this light from another lookout post, and sang out "Land ho!" – whereupon Columbus' page reprimanded him, saying: "My master has already seen it." [Oviedo's account.] The prearranged cannon-signal was not fired, however; since there had already been several false alarms, they were being cautious. The other two ships were also keeping a sharp lookout that night. Two hours after midnight the lookout on the *Pinta's* forecastle – Rodrigo de Triana, a sailor from Seville – "saw a shoreline of white sand, blinked his eyes, and cried out 'Land, land!' " [Testimony of García Vallejo at the trial.] Martín Pinzón immediately fired a cannon signal, and Columbus hailed him: "Señor Martín Alonso, you have found land. I shall give you five thousand *maravedis'* reward." As a matter of fact, it was Columbus himself who claimed the annuity of ten thousand *maravedis* offered by the Crown as a reward (which went to Beatriz de Harana). Did Rodrigo de Triana ever get his just reward? We do not know. This was an unjustice, certainly; but we must attribute it not to Columbus' cupidity, but rather to a proud self-regard stemming from religious considerations. As Las Casas, who consistently views history from a providentialist bias, later wrote: "It was proper that the reward should go to that one man who had always kept faith, to him who had first seen the light of this land, the symbol of that spiritual light he was destined to bring to it."

The shoreline grew more and more distinct, and there was general rejoicing. The crew of the *Santa María* crowded about their captain. "Some embraced him, others kissed his hands, begging him to forgive them their little faith." [Oviedo, II, 5.] At sunrise on October 12, 1492, the three vessels dropped anchor off the beach that forms the west face of the coral island of Guanahaní. A crowd of natives, naked from head to foot and daubed with streaks of paint of several colors, ran down to the sandy shore straightway. The three Captains took their places in the ships' boats – Columbus bearing the royal banner of Castile, and Martín and his brother Vicente standards with a green cross and the initials of Ferdinand and Isabella.

> Leaping out upon the shore, they kneeled and kissed it with tears of thanksgiving, thanking God who had rewarded them after a voyage so long and so strange – Columbus above all, for he was ever one to ponder the meaning of events, and in this moment saw his every hope confirmed.
>
> [Las Casas, I, 40.]

The Captain-General then rose to his feet, and gave to this land he had miraculously discovered the name of the Saviour: *San Salvador* (the name it still bears today). Meanwhile the crew and the royal officers also disembarked. Columbus then took solemn possession of the island in the name of the King and Queen of Castile, in the presence of the Fleet Secretary, Rodrigo de Escobedo. He then received from his company an oath of fealty to him as Admiral and Viceroy.

> What tongue can tell the honor given him, the forgiveness asked him, the obedience promised him! They were as if beside themselves, and with tears in his eyes he embraced them all and pardoned them, calling upon them to give the glory unto God.
>
> [Las Casas, I, 40.]

76

*Christopher Columbus lands.*
*(Théodore de Bry,* Americae pars IV, *Frankfurt, 1594.)*

We can well imagine the mutual stupefaction that both
Spaniards and Indians must have felt when they first laid
eyes on each other: the Indians stark naked, "with hair
that hung straight down, tall and erect in stature, with
skin the same color as that of the inhabitants of the
Canary Islands" [Columbus' journal], the Spaniards
bearded and heavily clothed.

It seemed at first as if they had come upon some
idyllic paradise:

> The Indians approached the Christians as children
> come unto their fathers; they were as naked as the
> day their mothers bore them, as if they had returned
> to that state of innocence wherein our father Adam
> dwelt.
>
> [Las Casas, I, 40.]

77

Columbus noted in his journal:

In order that we might win the friendship of these people (for I knew that love, not force, would bring them to our Holy Faith), I gave some of them colored caps and glass beads that they hung about their necks, taking much pleasure therein, and they showed us an affection so great that we marveled. Whereupon they swam out to the ships' boats where we were, bringing us parrots, little balls of cotton thread, paddles, and many other things which they exchanged for beads and hawks' bells. They most graciously gave us all they had. They seemed to me, however, to be a people that possessed no riches whatsoever. . . . They did not bear arms, nor did they have any knowledge of them, for I showed them some sabers and they took hold of them by the blade and cut themselves through knowing no better. . . . They immediately parrot everything said to them. I believe that they could easily be converted, for they appear to me to have no religion.

We here see at its source, we might add, the "myth of the noble savage," which was to enjoy such success in European literature.

The Admiral – for we may now refer to him by this title – realized immediately that he was not in Cypango, for on this flat, verdant, wooded island there was no sign of palaces with roofs of gold. But Marco Polo had also spoken of countless islands all around Japan. "According to the globes and illustrated world-maps that I have seen, Cypango is in this region." [Columbus' journal.] Shortly after his arrival, having admired certain native crafts – dugout canoes "most wondrously carved" and lengths of woven cotton – Columbus made inquiries about precious metal:

I paid close heed and tried to find out if there were gold about. I saw some men wearing a small bit of gold hanging from their noses; through their gestures they gave me to understand that by going south we would come upon a king who had golden vessels.

The ships weighed anchor on October 14, having taken aboard seven natives – who came along willingly – to help tame their coreligionists in other islands. Columbus' journal here contains the following disquieting passage:

> I shall later bring them back to Spain to teach them our language. Their Majesties could, moreover, have them all shipped off or keep them all captive, for with a force of fifty men they could be made to do what one pleased.

This is said ingenuously. . . .

The first island encountered at the southwest received the name of *Santa María de la Concepción* – a name that reveals Columbus' special devotion to the mystery of the Immaculate Conception, much revered by the Franciscans but still the object of violent controversy in other religious orders. The Admiral now cruised among the Bahamas for two weeks. The next two islands were named after Ferdinand and Isabella. He was quite sure that he was close to the continent of Asia; on October 17, the word "Indies" is mentioned in passing: "All these past days since I have been in the Indies, it has rained a bit." In Columbus' time the Antilles still had a dense covering of vegetation (which today has disappeared for the most part), and this wild beauty delighted him. (A "feeling for nature" is here evoked for the first time – in a travel-account at least.) At *Isabela* (today called *Crooked Island*) he writes, on October 21:

> Though the other islands I have already seen were most beautiful, this one is more beautiful still. There are great lagoons, and the whole forest round about is a marvel. The grass is like that of Andalusia in the month of April; and the song of the birds makes one want to stay here forever: flocks of parrot darken the sky in their flight; and there are, finally, trees of a thousand varieties, each with its own fruit, and all so fragrant that it is a marvel.

On October 25, he writes:

> I am about to set sail for another great island which

must be Cypango, if I judge rightly from what the Indians aboard tell me; they call it Colba [Cuba], and say that there are many ships there.... My plan, then, is to go to the Mainland and to the city of Quinsay, to present the letters from Your Majesties to the Grand Khan and bring back his reply.

On October 28, the three caravels anchored off the north coast of Cuba, which was named *Juana* in honor of the Infante Juan. The Admiral must have felt some disappointment on seeing no evidence of the heavy trade he had been led to expect, but he continued to trust his interpreters. "He thought that they had told him that the mainland lay ten days' journey away from this place." (How many gross misunderstandings must have resulted from the fact that the parties involved could express themselves only in sign-language!) He felt a bit disoriented nonetheless, and on October 29 noted that he "must make an attempt to go to the Grand Khan who he believed was to be found in this vicinity, or in the city of Cathay, according to what was told him before he left Spain." To clarify matters he decided on November 2 to send ambassadors to the king of the region. Concluding that he had made 1,142 leagues since leaving Ferro Island in the Canaries (a total error), he was certain that he was now on the coast of Asia; he therefore took one of the royal letters of credence, endorsed it over to Luis de Torres (the interpreter who knew Hebrew, Arabic, and Chaldaic) and Rodrigo de Xerez (who was acquainted with African dialects), and gave them two Indians as an escort.

But the envoys returned four days later, having found no trace of a civilized capital:

They reported that they had marched twelve leagues to a village of fifty dwellings.... The natives all touched them, kissed their hands and feet, and marveled, believing that they had descended from heaven. The leaders of the tribe took them in their arms and carried them to the chief's house and bade them sit down in two armchairs, while all squatted round about them.... The women felt them all over to see if they were made of flesh and bone like other men.

During their march they had crossed cultivated fields of sweet potatoes and maize (which at that time were unknown in Europe). What astonished them most of all was that "they had encountered many persons, men and women, going back to their villages with a lighted firebrand in their hand, with which they lighted herbs whose smoke they inhaled": this is none other than the first observed use of tobacco!

Columbus now made a change of plans. His guides had led him to believe, "by making gestures," that to the quarter east-northeast lay the island of Babeque, where "gold is gathered at night, by torchlight, and then hammered into bars," (a completely erroneous piece of information, we might add). He took his time nonetheless, ranging eastward along the coast of Cuba, for he wanted to discover how rich it was in spices, explore suitable sites for future Christian colonies, and prepare the way for the evangelization he so much desired. He writes:

> I hold it for a certainty that if we had sincere and devout Christian believers who knew their language, they would become converts forthwith. I hope that Your Majesties will attend to this most diligently, in order that so populous a nation may be turned to the Church and converted. [He has persuaded several natives to accompany him, and adds]: Thus they will learn our language, and adopt our customs and the articles of our Faith; for I see that these people have no religious practices and are not idolatrous, but rather are most docile and have no knowledge of evil, knowing neither how to kill nor how to take captives; they are so timid that a single one of our company can put a whole hundred of them to flight as a harmless jest. They know that there is a God on high, and are convinced that we have come from heaven. They parrot all the prayers that we recite, and make the sign of the cross.

On November 14, Columbus anchored in a bay studded with islands, to which he gave the name *Mar de Nuestra Señora* (the Sea of Our Lady – the present-day Tánamo Bay).

He marveled to see islands so numerous and so mountainous. . . . He writes that he believes these islands to be the countless islands shown on charts to lie at the farthest extremity of the Orient, and that there are hidden within them great treasures of precious stones and spices.

He took the time to have a great cross made from two large planks, and planted it at the entrance of the bay "in a lovely open spot on the heights, from which the view is most beautiful."

On November 19, he left the harbor under sail, setting a course north in the presumed direction of Babeque, but then changed course, believing that he had seen two islands in the distance (a mirage). On November 22, Martín Pinzón and the *Pinta* seized this chance to desert the tiny fleet – an act which in the Admiral's eyes constituted treason. The two remaining caravels continued to cruise along the coast of Cuba and were now approaching Haiti – to the great terror of the Indians on board:

They said that the inhabitants of this island had only one eye, in the middle of their forehead, and that there were others whom they called Cannibals. . . . They could speak no more, so afraid were they of being eaten.

(They were quite mistaken, as a matter of fact, for the ferocious Caribs lived farther south in the Lesser Antilles.) To the Admiral – still possessed by his *idée fixe* – the word *Caniba* sounded like *Grand Khan*. Since the Indians were "most cowardly" and had no arms, Columbus supposed it possible that the Grand Khan's men made raids on them. But their eating human flesh seemed to him to be no more than a tall tale: since these creatures made war, "they are beings endowed with reason" [entry in Columbus' journal, November 23] – a curious deduction!

On November 28, they reached another harbor, where they put in for several days because of bad weather. Their stay is described as follows:

It was most marvelous to see the fresh wooded groves, the crystal water, the birds, and all things so fair that it seemed to him that he would never be able to sail off again. He told his company that he would need more than a thousand tongues to tell the Sovereigns of all this.

The Admiral dreamed, of establishing a colony in this spot:

Your Majesties could command a city to be built here. The waters are fine and wholesome, not like those in Guinea, which are pestilential; not one of my men has had so much as a headache, or any sort of malady.... In these lands might be established a trading center for all Christendom and principally for Spain, which must be master of all. Only good Christian Catholics [i.e., no *conversos*] should be allowed to set foot here, for the prime purpose of this undertaking has always been the propagation and the glory of the Christian religion.

On December 4, the Admiral decided to leave Cuba (though he was not yet certain whether it was an island or "terra firma") and sail toward Babeque. But the wind came from the wrong quarter, and drove the caravels to the shores of nearby Haiti. On December 8, he anchored in the island's western bay, which he named *San Nicolás,* after the saint whose feast fell the following day – this is one of the rare names to have survived in modern nomenclature. Columbus now came upon one delightful spot after the other. On December 6, he entered a harbor which he named *Concepción,* for the next day was the Feast of the Conception of the Virgin.

He cast anchor in a river that was not very large; to the plains and countryside through which it flowed it imparted a wondrous beauty. A loach – exactly like the loaches in Spain – jumped up into the boat; he had not previously seen any species of fishes such as are found in Castile. He went some little distance inland in this region, which is all under cultivation, and heard the song of nightingales and other birds like those of Castile. He found myrtles and other trees similar of those of Castile.

The Admiral seems to have foreseen that this island would play a great role in his destiny. Because of the many points of similarity with Spain that he had noticed, he called it *Hispaniola* – the Spanish Isle.

Still hoping to reach Babeque, he now rounded the western cape of the island. The terrible cannibals were still much on his mind, and on December 10, he writes:

Again I say, as I have done many times before, that *Caniba* is none other than the land of the Grand Khan, which must be close by; he must have ships that come to take these natives captive; since the prisoners do not return, it is supposed that they have been eaten.

A great cross was erected on the heights of the promontory, "as a sign that Your Majesties are the possessors of these lands, and especially as a sign of Jesus Christ our Saviour, and the glory of Christianity." They now skirted the north coast of Haiti, sailing from west to east. Only one chart known to have been executed by Columbus has come down to us: it shows a portion of this very coast. It is drawn with a sure hand and is much closer to the truth than the chart drawn by Juan de la Cosa, the famous cosmographer.

Frequent landings were made, and the relations with the natives were excellent, since a "very young and very beautiful girl" came aboard; Columbus sent her back to shore, "most decorously, as was his habit," after giving her a necklace of glass beads and brass rings and clothing her. On December 15, they put in at the mouth of a river, a spot so lovely that Columbus called it *Valle del Paraíso* – the Valley of Paradise – and wrote: "I have never seen anything more beautiful." The next day brought an interview with a completely naked king who came down to the beach: "I sent him a present, which he accepted with great dignity. He appeared to be about twenty-one years of age, and was accompanied by a preceptor and other counselors." People in the king's retinue had little bits of gold leaf in their possession, and were quite willing to exchange them for trinkets. Columbus writes:

> Let Your Majesties be informed that Hispaniola is as much their possession as Castile; they need do nothing more than to have a settlement built here. . . . These people are most tractable, and easily led; they could be made to sow crops and build cities, and be taught to wear clothes and adopt our customs.

This program of colonization is set forth with naive frankness, but implies no conscious desire to harm the Indians: what could have been better for them than acceptance of the Christian way of life? . . .

The Admiral continued to beat to windward. On December 18, he dropped anchor in a harbor that he named *Nuestra Señora de la O,* in honor of that day's feast, the Annunciation of the Virgin. The young king (the first chieftain Columbus referred to by his native title of *cacique*) came aboard the flagship. Banners were unfurled and cannon volleys fired in honor of the fiesta. The scene as described in Columbus' journal is extremely colorful:

> There were more than two hundred men in the king's entourage; four of them bore him on a litter. While I was at table in the after-cabin he entered and at a brisk pace came to sit down beside me, nor would he permit me to rise. The thought came to me that he might care to taste our viands, and I gave orders for some to be brought to him. He gestured to his retinue to remain outside the cabin, which they did, all of them squatting on the deck, save two grown men whom I took to be his counselor and his preceptor, who came and seated themselves at his feet. He tasted of the dishes that I placed before him, then sent them to his people; he did the same with the wine, which he no more than raised to his lips. All this was done with wondrous dignity and few words; his two counselors kept their eyes full upon him, and spoke for him and with him most respectfully. After the

85

repast his attendant brought a girdle which he gave me, as well as two bits of fine-wrought gold; these were very thin, for it seems that they have but little gold here. I saw that a counterpane on my bed pleased him greatly; I gave it to him, along with a few strands of fine amber that I was wearing about my neck, some half-boots, and a flask of orange-flower water. He was so pleased therewith that I marveled. . . . I sent for a gold *excelente* on which are engraved the likenesses of Your Majesties; I showed it to him, and explained to him that Your Majesties have dominion over the better part of the world, and told him that there were no sovereigns greater. I showed him the royal banners and those which bear the cross, wherewith he was much impressed. What great sovereigns Your Majesties must be, he said, since they were not afraid to send [their Admiral] from so far a distance, indeed from heaven!

On December 20, he anchored in a harbor he named *Puerto Santo Tomás,* for it was the vigil of the Feast of Saint Thomas:

We caught sight of a very large valley, completely surrounded by very high mountains which seemed to touch the sky; beyond doubt these are mountains higher than those of the island of Tenerife in the Canaries, commonly held to be among the highest that can be seen.

His astonishment was so great that he feared he would be accused of exaggerating, and solemnly added:

I have sailed the sea for twenty-three years. . . . I have seen the Eastern Mediterranean, and the West toward the south; I have been to Guinea. But in all these waters there are no ports so perfect as these. . . . This port surpasses all others, and every ship in the world could be brought to harbor here at once, and the oldest hawser aboard be used to hold a ship at anchor with no danger whatsoever.

The Indians gave them as touching a welcome as they usually did:

> ... they bring us cassava bread, and offer us water in calabash-gourds and earthen pitchers of the same shape as those in Castile. ... And let it not be said that they give freely only that which is of little value, for they give away gold nuggets as willingly as they do a calabash of water; and it is easy to recognize when a thing is given from the heart.

A messenger came to the Admiral, sent by "the ruler of this whole land" – the famous Guacanagarí, who was to become the devoted friend of the Spaniards. The messenger brought him a valuable present: "a girdle which in the place of a buckle bore a mask with huge ears of beaten gold." The Admiral accepted the invitation extended him to visit the cacique. As they waited for a favorable wind for their departure, an unusually large crowd gathered about the two caravels: there were more than a thousand canoes, and each Indian bore a gift, among them many little gold nuggets. Columbus suspected that he was finally approaching a region where the precious metal was mined: "May Our Lord in His goodness guide me to this gold mine," he wrote feelingly – an emotion we quite understand in a man who had awaited this moment for more than two months. On December 24, an Indian named over for him all the places where gold was mined, and pronounced the name of *Cibao*; the Discoverer leaped to the conclusion that *Cibao* was *Cypango*!

Christmas was coming, and the Admiral was in high spirits. But that very day was to bring a wholly unforeseen shipwreck, which Columbus immediately took to be a providential event, for in all things he felt the need to see the hand of God. At nightfall on December 24, the two caravels were at sea, rounding a headland on their way to the bay close by where Guacanagarí was waiting for them. During the two days just past, no one aboard had been able to sleep, for the Indian visitors had swarmed all over the ship. When the 11 o'clock watch had been set Columbus – contrary to his habit – retired to his cabin to sleep. The sea was calm as oil and Juan de la Cosa, the ship's Master, deciding that he was not needed on deck, also retired to his cabin. Taking advantage of his absence, the helmsman turned the tiller over to a ship's boy. Toward midnight the boy – who could see nothing, and was not being conned by a pilot – felt the rudder of the *Santa María* touch bottom: the ship had grounded very gently, bow on, on a coral reef. He immediately called for help. The Admiral ordered the mate and a boat crew to run an anchor out astern to kedge the vessel off. But instead Juan de la Cosa, "to save his own skin," rowed off in the ship's boat to the *Niña*, which – fortunately – immediately lent a hand and sent its own ship's boat to pick up the men from the *Santa María*. Another boat was sent ashore to inform Guacanagarí of the disaster. The Indian canoes hurried out to unload the grounded vessel, with admirable discipline and dispatch. "Not so much as a needle was lost," Columbus wrote, and added, much touched:

> These are most loving people, who do not covet. They love their neighbor as themselves. They have a most gentle way of speaking, and have ever a pleasant smile. . . . They have no greed whatsoever for the property of others; this is particularly true of the King, who is most virtuous.

To console the Christians, the Indians brought them gold nuggets, and Guacanagarí offered his honored guests a banquet:

> . . . there was hutia, lobster, game, the bread they call cassava. . . . He wore a shirt and gloves the Admiral had given him, and he made more account of the gloves than of any other gift. From the way he ate, with dignified composure and beautifully refined table manners, it was evident that he was of noble birth. After the repast, grasses were brought to cleanse our hands.

Columbus then took his turn at entertaining, ordering one of his most skillful archers to shoot off showers of arrows; the lombard and a musket were also fired. A fine gift was offered him: a golden, jeweled mask, which he was to put over his face on the spot. This Christmas Day thus ended most auspiciously. Columbus decided to establish a colony on these hospitable shores, for it was, of course, quite impossible to take all his men home on the one vessel left him. Columbus writes:

There has been such concert amongst so many events that in truth it was not a disaster but a great good fortune. Had I not gone aground here, I would not have built a fortress. . . . I shall therefore leave behind a large company, eager to discover, in the service of Your Majesties, the mine from which the gold is taken. Thus all things have happened most opportunely. What it most remarkable is that when the ship ran aground it happened so gently that we did not even feel it, and there were no waves and no wind [another "sign" – like the incident of the "rough sea although there was no wind" of the outbound voyage]. When I return, my men will have been able to gather a barrel of gold and spices, so that three years hence Your Majesties may undertake the reconquest of the Holy House of Jerusalem.

Everyone was enthusiastic, and some thirty men offered to stay behind. (A year later not a single survivor was found.) A fort was soon raised, and named *Navidad* in memory of that Christmas Day. The little garrison was left with arms, a year's provisions, and the ship's boat so that they might explore the country. Diego de Harana, Beatriz' cousin, was to be in command.

Relations with the Indians were still excellent. Five "kings," tributaries of Guacanagarí, came to pay the Christians a visit:

One of them removed his crown from his own head and placed it on the Admiral's; the latter then took from his neck a necklace of fine colored stones, a most handsome piece of jewelry, and hung it about the King's neck; he then took off his mantle of fine scarlet and gave it to him; and placed, finally, a silver ring on his finger.

On January 2, 1493, Columbus re-embarked with half his men. Before taking leave of the Indians, he ordered men in combat dress to wage a sham-battle "to inspire in them a fear such as will keep them respectful." They left the little garrison behind with no foreboding.

On January 6, a happy event occurred: the *Pinta* reappeared over the horizon, and Martín Pinzón immediately came aboard the *Niña* to make his apologies to the Admiral for his long defection. "But his reasons were all false," Columbus writes. "When he parted company with me his only motives were insolence and greed. . . ." Pinzón wanted to take advantage of the greater speed of his ship to reach Babeque first and carry off the gold. "I concealed my dissatisfaction," Columbus continues, "in order not to further the works of Satan, who since the beginning had sought to hinder this voyage." The Genoese now thought only of sailing home as fast as possible to give the Sovereigns news of his discovery. The coast of Haiti stretched out before him to the east, but he did not linger to reconnoiter. On January 13, an encounter occurred that might have been disastrous: a party of seven men who had gone ashore to get fresh provisions had seen, behind the trees, a band of about fifty naked natives, with long hair and faces streaked with charcoal. Each of them was armed with bow and arrows; this was the first time that armed Indians had been encountered, and these seemed ready for battle. The Christians did not let their fear get the better of them; one of them slashed one of the Indians with a knife, and the Indians scattered. The pilot forbade his boat crew to chase them down and kill them. "I was glad on the one hand yet regretful on the other," Columbus writes, "for it would have been a good thing to inspire fear in them, especially if our men from Navidad should one day come this way." He concluded that these were the terrible *Caniba*, or Caribs, he had heard so much about.

The caravels then shaped a course for a mysterious *Isle of Women* (Martinique), which according to the natives was inhabited only by women and lay next to an island inhabited by men. Columbus would have very much liked to verify the truth of this tale, for it coincided exactly with Marco Polo's account of the islands of *Feminea* and *Masculina* in the Indian Ocean. But a freshening wind pushed the caravels northeast, the most favorable quarter for the homeward passage. He need only set the course for the ocean voyage, "putting all things in God's trust."

For three weeks things could not have gone better, and Columbus profited from this happy interval to draw up his famous report on the success of his enterprise.

The little fleet's course brought them up to the same parallel as the Bermudas – a latitude much farther south than that taken on the outbound passage – and they now caught the westerlies. On February 10, the fleet had reached the latitude of the Azores. On the twelfth a gale began to shape up, as frequently happens in this season in these waters. The entry in Columbus' log for February 14 reads:

> That night the wind rose and the waves were fearsome, with a cross-sea that stopped the *Niña's* headway in the swells. I set the main course on a yard slung very low, and let her run thus for three hours and twenty miles. I then let the caravel scud before the wind. The *Pinta* too began to run before the wind, and we lost sight of her during the night. At sunrise, the wind blew more violently still, and the sea grew fearsome. I then ran under bare poles so that the ship would not be swamped.

Lots were drawn three times for volunteers to go on pilgrimages if the ship's company escaped alive. On the first and third draw the lot fell to Columbus. The whole company pledged, moreover, that as soon as they reached land they would go to the nearest church in their shirts [as a sign of penance] to thank Our Lady.

Las Casas, who is consulting Columbus' own journal as he writes, says:

> The Admiral here enters the reasons that caused him to fear that Our Lord wished to see him perish, and those that caused him to hope, on the contrary, that God would save him. So great was his desire to bring the Sovereigns the news of his discovery and show that

he had not been wrong, that he was a little afraid that he would not be able to carry his purpose through; for, he writes, "the least little mosquito is enough to trouble me." [This nervous irritability is interesting to note.] He attributes this fear to his little faith in Divine Providence. But remembering on the other hand the graces God had granted him, remembering how He had fulfilled his every desire after the many adversities he had suffered in Castile, he felt himself comforted. Since God had rewarded him when he had trusted his plan unto Him, he had reason to believe that He would bring to fruition that which He had begun. God had aided him, moreover, on the outbound passage when his men were plotting mutiny against him, giving him the courage to stand against them; many wondrous things had been manifest in him and for him on this voyage; not to mention those things whereof Their Majesties already had knowledge. "But my weakness and my anguish were so great," the Admiral writes, "that my soul would not take courage." He thought too of his two sons, whom he had left in a foreign land. Fearing lest he perish before the news of his discovery reached the world, he drew up on a sheet of parchment a brief account of his voyage and the course he had followed. "This account," he wrote, "I send to Your Majesties sealed and signed, with the promise of a thousand ducats to any person presenting it to you still sealed; thus if foreigners found it, they could not make use of the information contained therein."

The parchment was then wrapped in a piece of waxed cloth, sealed in a barrel, and dropped overboard. No more was ever heard of it. . . .

On February 16, the wind died down a bit. Then:

As the *Salva Regina* was being sung, they saw a light from land. . . . That night the Admiral rested for a time, for he had not slept in four days, and could hardly move his legs, for he had been out in the cold and wet and had taken almost no food.

(It was at this time that Columbus incurred the

arthritis that was to cause him severe suffering.)

At sunrise on the eighteenth they anchored off the island of Santa María, a Portuguese possession in the Azores. Columbus' troubles were not yet ended. As dawn came up the following day, his first thought was to fulfill the promise made to God at the height of the storm. He put half his crew ashore to make their way to a little shrine that they could see a short distance off on a promontory; upon their return, he and the rest of the ship's company were to go off by the same path. At 11 a.m. none of the men had come back: the Governor of the island had set upon the unarmed men in order to secure a ransom from the Spanish caravel, for he suspected it of trespassing along the coast of Guinea, waters which only the Portuguese had the right to enter. Shortly thereafter the Governor, escorted by men-at-arms, came out to the *Niña* in a boat, but refused to come aboard. From over the bulwarks, Columbus showed him the letters of credence from the Sovereigns of Castile, and demanded that his men be released. "I have no fear of the King and Queen of Castile," the Governor insolently replied. Columbus was "most distressed, and wondered whether another war had broken out between Spain and Portugal; but he could not help replying as he saw fit." (We shall see this quick temper displayed on other occasions!) The two men parted amid mutual threats; but three days later the matter was settled, and the captured crew was freed and sent back aboard.

Columbus did not linger in these inhospitable waters in which he had already lost all too much time. The *Pinta* had disappeared in the storm, but it was presumed that she had been driven to the coast of Spain and would be the first to report the news of the discovery of the Indies – as was, in fact, the case. The *Niña* therefore laid a course for Cape St. Vincent; but another storm overtook her, and two of her sails were torn to pieces. On the night of March 3-4, land was sighted in the moonlight. "The sea raised the caravel in the air, and lightning flashed on all sides. We waited for daylight amid endless anxiety and anguish." The land sighted was the Roca de Sintra, near Lisbon. The *Nina* dropped anchor inside the Tagus estuary, in the harbor of Lisbon.

Columbus had thus entered the territory of the King of Portugal, whose temporary court was nine leagues away. Columbus' first step was to write the King to try to disarm his ill-feeling:

> I informed him that I had received from the Sovereigns of Castile the strict order to enter a Portuguese port and there seek what I needed, offering payment in return. My prime purpose was to inform him that I was returning not from Guinea, but from the Indies.

That same day he added a postscript to his report to Ferdinand and Isabella:

> After having written this and entered Spanish waters, a storm drove me to tie up today in this port of Lisbon. . . . Everyone here agrees that there has never been a winter so bad as this one, nor so many vessels lost.

Moored alongside the shabby-looking little caravel with torn sails was a magnificent Portuguese man-of-war, fitted out with an impressive battery of cannon. Its master was none other than Bartholomeu Dias, the discoverer of the Cape of Good Hope, whom Columbus had met several years before. Dias asked the Captain of the foreign sailing vessel to report aboard the warship to show his credentials. The Genoese immediately stood on his dignity, again showing that same hauteur that had kept the Governor of Santa María at a respectful distance:

> He replied that he was an Admiral of the Sovereigns of Castile, and accounted to no one . . . and that it was the habit of Admirals of Castile to die rather than surrender themselves or their men. The master took a more moderate tone and said that if this were his pleasure, his wish would be respected; but he asked him to show him the credentials from the Sovereigns of Castile. This the Admiral deigned to do.

The master and the Captain of the warship then

came to pay Columbus a courtesy visit, to the sound of trumpets and fifes.

For three days there were continual festivities aboard, for the Lisboners came in droves to see the Indians – the wretched, naked Indians who must have suffered even more than the others in the course of the rough crossing. "All gave infinite thanks to Our Lord for having brought so large a flock to the fold of Christ." At the cordial invitation of John II, Columbus then went ashore to go to the royal residence, "though I did so against my will."

Columbus' entry in his journal describing the reception given him is brief. He shows only the bright side: the honor extended him when the King bade him sit down with him; the "gracious mien" of the King, "who expressed great pleasure that this voyage had ended so well." But Dom João's conversation augured ill for the future; he claimed that everything that had been discovered belonged to him in virtue of the peace treaty with the Sovereigns of Castile – in his view the exclusive sphere of influence granted him on the coasts of West

*The four voyages of Columbus.*

Africa also included the Ocean Sea touching those shores on the west. Like his host, the Genoese was careful not to show his hand too openly, and said only that he had obeyed the orders of his Sovereigns to the letter and had carefully abstained from going to Guinea. Las Casas gives further details [I, ch. 74], which are corroborated by Ruy de Pina, the royal chronicler of the Court of Portugal. He describes the impression that the Indians Columbus presented at court made on Dom João (they had outlined a map of the Antilles for him, using dried beans); the monarch's rage when he saw so many lands slipping through his fingers; the plan to assassinate the Genoese that was proposed to the King, to which he did not give his consent. "All this the Admiral passes over in silence in his Journal, for these were things to be told in private, when he had been granted audience with the Sovereigns." [Las Casas.]

Columbus then went back to Lisbon. Having been made seaworthy once again, the *Niña* weighed anchor on March 13. At noon on the fourteenth she crossed the bar at Saltés at flood tide and put into the port òf Palos, from where she had sailed on August 3 of the preceding year. Columbus was now to enjoy six months of un-clouded glory.

A first stroke of good luck – if we may call it that – immediately befell him: Martín Pinzón, his potential rival, disappeared from the scene. Driven by the storm, the *Pinta* had made port, not in the Azores as the *Niña* had, but along the coast of Galicia; Pinzón had written from there to the sovereigns, then at their order had set sail for Palos, arriving – by a curious coincidence – on the same day as Columbus, a few hours later. Exhausted by the weeks of hardship he had undergone, mortified by his rival's triumph, Martín took to his bed as soon as he arrived home and died within the month.

Ferdinand and Isabella had already received the letter Columbus had sent from Portugal. The tone of the letter was calculated to arouse their enthusiasm:

> I arrived in the Indies in seventy-one days, and found there numerous islands, whereof I took possession in the name of Their Majesties, finding no

impediment thereunto. The first I called *San Salvador,* in honor of the Divine Lord, Who miraculously granted all this unto me. . . . The peoples of all the islands I have seen – both the men and the women – go about quite naked. They know not the use of iron, and have no arms; they are well-proportioned and tall in stature, but are extraordinarily timid; when I chanced to send two or three men ashore to speak with them, they took flight forthwith despite their numbers; yet no harm was ever done them. But once their fear has left them, they give proof of an innocence and a generosity that can scarcely be believed. No matter what is asked of them, they never refuse it, and show themselves content with any gift offered them. . . . I gave them many a pretty little trinket in order that they might conceive an affection for us; for in this fashion they will soon be converted to our Christian faith, and drawn to the love and service of Their Majesties; they will freely give us all those things they so abundantly possess. They have no religious practices, and no idolatry; their one belief is that the sky is the seat of all power and all good; they firmly believe that I and my men came from heaven in our ships; this they believe because they have never seen men wearing clothing, nor ships such as ours. . . . In the first island that I reached I had a few natives brought aboard to tell me of these lands. Wherever I went, they would call out: "Come see the men who dwell in heaven!" And all would flock round about us – men, women, and even little children – each bringing us whereof to eat or drink, presenting their gifts with wondrous signs of affection. . . . In all these islands I noticed almost no differences of custom or of language; they all understand each other – a most singular phenomenon which I hope will incline Their Majesties to undertake converting them to our Christian faith. . . . It appears to me that in all these islands the men have no more than one wife, save the King, who has as many as twenty. The women labor harder than the men. It seems to me that they have no property of their own, but share everything in common. I encountered no monsters, though there were many who held that such existed there. They are people of noble bearing, and they are not black like the natives of Guinea. I have heard it said, however, that there is an island wherein dwell a most ferocious people who devour human flesh. But they are no more mis-shapen than are the others; it is simply that they wear their hair long, as women do, and use bows and arrows with a hollow reed for a tip. . . . There is abundant gold in Hispaniola, as the Indians that I am bringing back with me can testify . . . there are also spices, cotton, mastic such as is found only in Greece and on the island of Chios, and aloes wood; there are likewise slaves, that could be taken from among the idolatrous; I also believe that I found rhubarb and cinnamon. . . . All this is certain fact. In this enter-prise that seemed impossible, our Lord God has made me to prosper, as He does all those who follow in His ways. Although others spoke of these lands, it was but conjecture, for they had not seen them; and thus those who heard of this undertaking thought it a mere fiction. . . . Thus hath Our Redeemer brought victory unto our illustrious King and Queen, wherefore all Christendom ought to rejoice and give thanks unto the Holy Trinity, seeing the many souls that will have been brought to our Christian faith.

To attest to this discovery made in the name of the Crown of Castile, the Sovereigns ordered this epistle (known as the *Letter to Santangel, the Royal Treasurer*) printed immediately. In order to give it an international audience, they also had it translated into Latin by a Catalan attached to the court of Pope Alexander VI; this first edition appeared in Rome at the beginning of May, 1493, and was subsequently reprinted many times. The sovereigns faced, indeed, the urgent need to fortify them-selves against possible claims on the part of Portugal.

Immediately following his return to Palos, Columbus wrote the Sovereigns again. The royal reply, dated March 30, addressed him for the first time by the glorious titles of Admiral of the Ocean Sea, Viceroy, and Governor; the letter enjoined him to present himself at court with-out delay and to begin preparations for another voyage immediately. Columbus promptly drafted a proposal for colonization: constructing cities in the New World, sending priests to convert the Indians and Crown comptrollers to supervise the collection of gold. This is the first document on which there appears the mysterious set of initials which no researcher has yet deciphered satisfactorily:

.  S  .
.  S  .  A  .  S  .
X    M    Y

followed by the signature *XPo Ferens* ("Christo ferens"): "the Christ-Bearer" – a paraphrase of his name.

We now find Columbus in Seville, with members of his crew and the ten Indians transplanted from their far-off island homeland. They attracted great crowds of Sevillans. Bartholomew de Las Casas, who was then a child, was later to remember seeing this picturesque little band, who had been given lodgings "near the arch called *Las Imágenes,* in the quarter of San Nicolás," and the extraordinary fiestas that were held, "like those on Corpus Christi, unforgettable in their novelty and solemn splendor."

Columbus could not tarry long. He passed through Córdova, met there Beatriz de Harana and his two sons, whom he had left in her care, and rode on toward Barcelona with a small escort of royal cavaliers and seven of his Indians, bearing vividly colored parrots and the finest of the gifts he owed to the generosity of the Indian caciques.

The reception at court was magnificent:

The streets could not hold the multitudes that poured forth; all were overwhelmed with admiration when they saw this venerable person who was said to have discovered a New World, when they saw the Indians, the parrots, the many mementos and golden jewels and all manner of things they had never before heard of. . . . The Admiral entered the hall where the Sovereigns, the Infante Juan, and a great crowd of caballeros and hidalgos were waiting. Among this noble assembly his lofty stature and his air of authority, his noble countenance crowned by his white hair, his modest smile gave him the appearance of a Roman senator. The Sovereigns rose, as they would for a great nobleman, and when he had kissed their hands they bade him rise, then with most gracious countenance ordered that a chair be brought and had him sit between them on the dais. When he had given wise account of all the graces God had given unto him during his voyage, and of the grandeur and felicity of the lands discovered; when he had displayed the pieces of carved gold and the specimens of gold, some in large nuggets and some in fine grains, and avowed that these lands produced such in infinite quantities; when he had described the innocence and docility of these peoples and their readiness to receive our Holy Faith – as was well proven by the Indians that he had brought thence – then the Sovereigns rose and kneeled, their eyes full of tears, and the choir of the royal chapel chanted the *Te Deum*.

[Las Casas, I, ch. 79.]

(Too young to have been there himself, Las Casas is here following the account of Oviedo, the royal chronicler, who had witnessed the whole ceremony.)

Religious instruction of the Indians began immediately – we wonder in what language! – and they were baptised a month later, with the King, the Queen, and the Infante Juan and others serving as godparents. Very few of the Indians survived this total change of climate and way of life; one of those who did survive was Diego Colón, a native of San Salvador, who was baptised Diego in honor of the Admiral's brother; for several years he was to render valuable service as an interpreter.

The Admiral now enjoyed the highest honors. He rode at the King's side, a rare privilege ordinarily granted only to persons of royal blood. The Grand Cardinal of Spain invited him to dine, gave him the place of honor beside him, and served him dishes that he had tasted beforehand. It is quite probable that the Genoese concealed his plebeian origins – an understandable temptation –

at the time that he was granted the privilege of placing on his escutcheon the arms of Castile and Leon, "reserving for the base your own arms, those that you are accustomed to bear." He was raised to the Spanish nobility, and thus enjoyed the right to be addressed as *Don,* a privilege also extended to his two brothers – Bartholomew, who was then in France, and Giacomo (known as *Diego* in Castilian), who was still in Genoa – a detail which serves to prove that he neither neglected nor disavowed his family. He obtained at the same time solemn confirmation of the *Capitulations.*

How gratified he must have been to see that views of his which had once been dismissed as idle dreams had now found complete acceptance! "The more we understand the grandeur of your plan," the Sovereigns wrote him, "the more we esteem the wisdom you have displayed, a wisdom we would not have supposed any mortal to possess." Learned scholars were not the last to be wildly enthusiastic. Peter Martyr d'Anghiera for instance – a young Italian humanist in the service of the Court of Castile – wrote his correspondents after meeting the Genoese:

Columbus had just returned from the Western Antipodes. [Letter of May 14.]

What an admirable discovery! And so it comes to pass that that which had been unknown since the very creation of the world is now beginning to be revealed. . . . Columbus has just discovered a new hemisphere of the earth, lying in the Western Antipodes. [Letter of September 13.]

Peter Martyr now began to compose his *Decades,* the first of which was entitled *De orbe novo* [*On the New World*]. The adjective *new* must not be misinterpreted here: for Peter Martyr, as for Columbus, *new world* meant a part of Asia which was still unknown to Europeans but was nonetheless to be considered a part of the "Indies." They did not yet suspect that a new continent had been discovered.

It was imperative that the Pope, the highest spiritual

authority, be asked to ratify the formal ceremony of possession of the Indies that had taken place in the name of Castile. It was the Papacy that in 1418 had granted the Crown of Portugal the right to extend its sovereignty "beyond the Canary Islands, toward Guinea." (The term *beyond* was very vague, for it could be interpreted to mean either *to the west or to the south.*) The new Pope, Alexander VI, was a Spanish Borgia who was on intimate terms with Ferdinand and Isabella: it was he who gave them the title of *Their Catholic Majesties.* As early as May 4, the Pontiff recognized the discovery of islands "toward the Indies" whose inhabitants seemed most deserving of Christian conversion, and gave the right of sovereignty to the Crown of Castile "on condition that they send thence wise and learned men to instruct the natives in the Christian doctrine." Immediately upon his arrival in Barcelona, Columbus insisted that the terms of the grant of sovereignty be spelled out in detail. From this there resulted a second papal bull, entitled *Inter caetera,* establishing an imaginary line of demarcation a hundred leagues west of the Azores: west of the line, all expeditions and the profit therefrom were to be the exclusive right of the Sovereigns of Castile (and beyond this line the jurisdiction of the Admiral of the Ocean Sea was also to begin); east of the line, the Portuguese were to enjoy exclusive rights. In that era no one questioned the Pope's right to delegate temporal power – to be exercised for spiritual ends, naturally. Columbus – who had taken possession of the lands he had discovered both in the name of Christ and that of the Crown of Castile – would have been the last to distinguish spiritual powers from temporal.

The Crown of Portugal did not immediately accept the papal decree, and appeared to be assembling a large flotilla in the Azores. A year later (June, 1494) the Treaty of Tordesillas was signed. Through direct negotiations between the two Courts John II received an important concession: the line of demarcation was moved back to fall on the meridian 370 leagues west of the Cape Verde Islands (and thus Brazil when it was discovered fell automatically within the Portuguese zone). It is possible, as A. Cioranescu suggests, that the so-called

"Toscanelli correspondence" was forged in Lisbon in the course of these difficult negotiations, for the purpose of establishing that the Crown of Portugal had had the idea of "reaching the East by sailing west" long before the Crown of Castile, and that Columbus had more or less stolen the idea. Columbus at this point had again sailed off to the Indies and thus could not deny the accusation. (He allegedly learned of the forged documents on his return in 1496, whereupon he copied the "letter to Martins" on the end-papers of the *Historia rerum.*) But we might object to Cioranescu's hypothesis on these grounds: Why did Columbus refrain from mentioning the matter later? And why did Portuguese chroniclers never mention this accusation?

The preparations for the second voyage were concluded in a matter of weeks, having been handed over to a newly created officer of the Crown: Archdeacon Juan Rodríguez de Fonseca, "Superintendent of the Affairs of the Indies" – he was an excellent administrator, but he and Columbus were never to get along together. The royal instructions, which had been drawn up along lines suggested by the Admiral, constituted a complete plan for colonization. Hundreds of men appointed by the Crown were to go off to the Indies as settlers: hidalgos, who were to provide their own horses; day laborers (bricklayers and miners), farmers. (There were no women however.) Newborn animals – mares, ewes, sheep – were also taken, Peter Martyr tells us in his *First Decade,* for the only quadrupeds that had been found in the Antilles were "mute dogs." Wheat and oat seeds, cuttings of grapevines, and seedlings were also taken. Many provisions were loaded on board, and a customshouse was established in Cádiz to register the cargoes shipped. The Crown was to have a trade monopoly, to which the Admiral was to contribute one-eighth of the expenses and receive a corresponding profit – as had been stipulated in the *Capitulations.* A fifth of the gold was to be set aside for the Royal Treasury. As Governor, Columbus was to have the power to appoint all officials, subject to the Crown's approval.

The religious objective was clearly outlined, as were

the means to be employed in proselytizing: "The Indians must be treated lovingly, in order that they may be tamed." This time there was a Chaplain of the Fleet aboard: a Benedictine monk, Fray Bernardo Buil, who played a large part in ruining Columbus' reputation and made almost no effort to convert the Indians. There were four others monks: three "Burgundian" Franciscans and a Spanish Jeronymite, Fray Ramón Pane.

The fleet consisted of seventeen ships, with a complement of about twelve hundred men. Diego Columbus, Christopher's younger brother, sailed with him: "a virtuous man, simple of heart and guileless, who wore the habit of a cleric." [Las Casas.] The father and uncle of Bartholomew de Las Casas also sailed with the armada, the latter as Captain of the armed forces. (For his account of the next years our historian of the Indies thus had at his disposal both information transmitted to him orally and the Admiral's shipboard journal, which has since been lost.) The future conquistador Alonso de Hojeda was also aboard. There was a physician, Dr. Chanca; he was a chronicler as well, and left us an account of this voyage. There was no official cosmographer, but among the able seamen was a man destined to become a famous cartographer: Juan de la Cosa. (He must not be confused – as he usually is – with a man of the same name who was the pilot of the Santa María.)

Most of the crew came from the Andalusian coast, and many of them had sailed with Columbus on the first voyage. But there were also a few Genoese, among them one of Columbus' childhood friends, Michele de Cuneo, who also left us an account of the expedition.

The Admiral of the Ocean Sea, Captain-General of a rather imposing flotilla, had reached the height of his glory as the seventeen vessels sailed majestically out of the harbor of Cádiz on September 25, 1493, their banners full unfurled; no period of his life was ever again to be as happy.

104

*The islands discovered, as shown on the chart of Juan de la Cosa, 1500.*

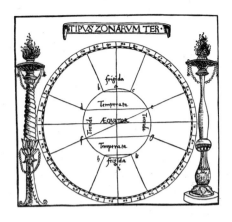

# THE RETURN TO THE NEW WORLD

The first port of call was the Canary Islands, as it had been the year before. The Admiral then took a more southerly rhumb than on the first voyage, for he was setting a course for that part of the archipelago south of Hispaniola that the Indians had pointed out to him. Less than a month later, after a perfect crossing, the armada entered the Caribbean Sea. The first island sighted was named *Dominica* (Santo Domingo) for the landfall had been made on a Sunday. They then ranged the whole semicircular chain of islands. The sea was sweet scented, and Columbus must have again recalled the perfumed islands of the Cypango Sea that Marco Polo had mentioned.

But their admiration soon turned to horror, for they encountered proof of the cannibalism of the fierce Carib warriors: on Guadeloupe (an island which was named after the famous shrine in Extremadura) the Spaniards found remains of roast cuts of human flesh, and delivered captives doomed to this gruesome fate. In another island the Christians had a hand-to-hand combat with the savage *Caniba,* several of whom were taken prisoner.

On November 24, 1493, Columbus found that he had again reached the eastern extremity of Haiti, from which

*Indians, "armed and hostile." (Théodore de Bry).*

he had set his course for Spain the year before on January 16. He now sailed on as fast as possible to rejoin the thirty-nine Christians he had left at the fort of Navidad. On the twenty-seventh the caravels anchored off the site of the fort. Las Casas writes:

> Toward the middle of the night a canoe full of Indians approached the flagship, shouting "Admiral, Admiral!" He appeared on deck and they recognized him straightway by his tall stature. They came aboard and gave him masks inlaid with gold as presents from King Guacanagarí. The Admiral inquired after the Christians, for he was most anxious about them. They replied that some had sickened and died, and others had gone off with women.... The next day the Admiral went ashore at Navidad and saw that the fortress had been burned to the ground. Seeing no sign of anyone, he realized that all those he had left there, all those from whom they had taken their leave in such joy and satisfaction, were now dead, and a great sadness filled his heart.
>
> [Las Casas, I, ch. 85-86.]

Seven or eight bodies of dead Spaniards were found. The Indians did not come out of hiding, but Guacanagarí's brother, accompanied by natives who knew a little Castilian, came to speak with Columbus. He reported (and it is quite likely that his account of what had happened was true) that as soon as the Admiral had sailed away, the Christians had disbanded to search for gold; arriving in the territory of a king named Caonabó, they had extorted tribute in gold and carried off the women. Being of a less peaceful disposition than Guacanagarí, Caonabó had avenged himself by killing these scattered men (whom the Indians at first considered immortal), and had then come to Navidad on a punitive expedition and set fire to the fortress. Had Guacanagarí been an accomplice? He maintained that he was ill from a wound he had received while defending the Christians, but Dr. Chanca noticed that the wound was quite imaginary.

Columbus' officers – especially Fray Buil, the Chaplain of the Fleet – were of the opinion that an exemplary

*The Indians put the "immortality" of the Spaniards to the test.*
*(Théodore de Bry, Americae pars IV).*

punishment should be meted out to the cacique. But the
Admiral refused to consent to this, for as Las Casas
writes, citing Columbus:

> ... acting in this wise would neither bring the dead
> back to life nor send them unto Heaven – if they were
> not already there. Furthermore, this would bring on
> a war, and the Sovereigns sent me here to establish a
> colony, and they have disbursed much money to that
> purpose; and above all it would be a great hindrance
> to the conversion of these people to our Holy Faith,
> which is the principal aim of this undertaking.

This disaster was to prove a great handicap. They had
expected to find a small nucleus of Christians in a permanent colony, who would already have explored the
countryside round about and discovered the gold mines

109

of Cibao. The attempt to colonize had thus begun most inauspiciously, and when the aniversary of their first Christmas came round – that Christmas that Columbus had thought was a miracle – it must have required a heroic act of faith still to believe that the shipwreck of the year before, in this very spot, had been expressly willed by Providence! In any event, a colony at Navidad was now out of the question; they would have to find a site closer to the gold mine that had so raised their hopes. The fleet again sailed eastward on December 7, and anchored in the first promising spot: a little plain with a stream flowing through it. "I decided to build my colony there, in the name of the Holy Trinity." The site had wood and stone, and the workmen could begin building immediately. This was *Isabela* – so named in honor of Queen Isabella – the first Christian settlement in the New World. They set themselves immediately to building a church, and soon, on January 6, 1494, the mass of consecration was held. It was the Feast of the Epiphany, which celebrates the universality of salvation – a fitting prelude to their apostolic mission! But in the years that followed no one except Columbus and Fray Ramón Pane apparently bothered to bring the Glad Tidings to the Indians.

The Admiral now plunged into the problems of governing the island – in particular the difficult task that fell to him as founder of a colony. When at sea, Columbus was always able to control events. But he was to be overwhelmed by the problems involved in colonizing the New World. His greatest burden was the financial side of the enterprise, the desire to show a rapid and substantial profit to balance the huge sums (including the salaries of some twelve hundred colonists) that had been paid out by the Crown; this he hoped to do largely by collecting gold, that object of so many of his glowing promises.

From the very first days the whole colony, including the Admiral, fell ill. Most of the newly arrived colonists were landsmen, whom the voyage and the many hardships had greatly exhausted. It would be futile to see in this fact the first appearance of syphilis. As Morison remarks:

110

The history of American colonization proves that you cannot land a body of men after a long ocean voyage, subject them to hard labor with inadequate housing in torrential rains, expose them to mosquitoes full of germs with which their systems are unprepared to cope, and feed them on fish, maize, yams and cassava instead of beef, pork, wheat bread and wine, without excessive sickness and great mortality.[1]

Columbus himself had to take to his bed for a time, since, as Las Casas writes:

> ... his fatigue during the time that he was leading the fleet had been considerable; not only had he not had the opportunity to sleep, as is always true of those who are pilots ... but also he had in his care a whole fleet, in waters that no one knew; and above all, he knew that the world was waiting to see the result of his undertaking, and felt himself obliged to fulfill the desires of the Sovereigns of Castile and all Christendom ... and at each moment he had all these things much upon his mind.
>
> [Las Casas, I, ch. 89.]

On January 30, Columbus sent twelve ships back to Spain, under the command of Antonio de Torres, to whose care he entrusted a long memorandum for the sovereigns (the original of which, in Columbus' own hand, with the marginal annotations added by Ferdinand and Isabella, has been preserved.) In it he makes a great point of the hopes he has of finding the gold mine in the near future; he also describes at length the destitution of the inhabitants of Isabela, who are sick, have no medicines, and lack sufficient supplies. But time will remedy their situation:

> This year we sowed few crops, for the few laborers we have fell ill. ... The wheat and the grape vines will produce a good harvest; this land seems wondrously fertile, and will easily be the equal of Andalusia and Sicily insofar as sugar cane is concerned.

---

[1]   Morison, *ibid.*, p. 434.

He then discusses the question of the cannibals, for there had been some captured in the Caribbean archipelago:

> ... it seems to me that only good can come from sending them off to Castile in order that they may at last give up their inhuman custom of eating people, and learn our language and thus be more inclined to receive baptism. We will gain great prestige, moreover, among the people here when they see us capture those who bring them such great harm.

Columbus naturally sanctioned the enslavement of inferior beings such as these. But he went farther still: since caravels would have to make regular voyages back and forth between the colony and the mother country, since the settlement would need to be supplied with livestock, provisions, and seed, he calmly proposed loading cannibal slaves aboard, who would then be sold in Spain. Columbus' espousal of slavery was forever to stand in the way of his canonization (though Roselly de Lorgues attempted in the last century to institute proceedings in Rome to have Columbus elevated to sainthood, a cause that enlisted Léon Bloy's impassioned support). Worse still, it was not only the savage Caribs who were to be enslaved, but also the docile Indians of Hispaniola, after despair later drove them to armed revolt.

On March 12, Columbus too set out to explore the region, leading a troop of heavily armed men, "with their banners full unfurled, sounding their trumpets, and firing musket volleys." It was an exhausting cavalcade. They finally reached a certain pass from which they could see a fertile valley. As Las Casas writes, following Columbus' lost journal:

> [This valley was] so fine and verdant that it seemed to them that they were in some region of Paradise. The Admiral, who sought in all things their deepest meaning, gave infinite thanks unto God and gave it the name of *Vega Real* [the Royal Plain].
> [Las Casas, ch. 90.]

After crossing many gold-bearing rivers, Columbus chose a well-protected little mesa as the site on which to build an earthen fort. Las Casas tells us:

> He called it the fortress of Santo Tomás, in memory of the disbelief of Saint Thomas the Apostle, for his men would not believe that there was gold in this island until they had touched it with their own hands.
> [Las Casas, ch. 91.]

But such disbelief now became impossible, for the natives brought them enormous gold nuggets. A garrison of fifty men was left behind under the command of an Aragonese nobleman, Pedro Margarit; Margarit's orders were to explore the region, but being a hard-bitten old soldier he seriously compromised the effort to enter the region peaceably. The instructions that the Viceroy left him were a model of Christian moderation, but they set up no supply system and thus Margarit and his men could not avoid "living off the land." Columbus' orders read:

> The essential thing is to be most careful that no harm be done the Indians; on the contrary, let them be honored and made to feel secure, so that they may have no reason to be irritated. . . . Their Majesties prefer the salvation of these people and their conversion to all the riches that might be found here.

But strong measures were recommended in certain cases:

> If certain of them commit thefts, chastise them by cutting off their ears and noses. In this wise all inhabitants of this island will know that the wicked are punished whereas the righteous are well-treated.

This was a cruel mode of punishment – though it was also applied in Castile – and Captain Hojeda did not hesitate to bring it to bear on an Indian accused of stealing clothing. The whole affair went even farther: the cacique of the region was captured and sent to

113

Isabela; Columbus was about to put him to death, then changed his mind at the last moment.

Things were going very badly at Isabela: there were epidemics and famine, for the food supplies soon rotted in the damp climate. To get fresh flour a dam and a gristmill had to be built along the stream. Since the workmen had all fallen ill, Columbus pressed the hidalgos into service. "But they considered working with their hands a fate as cruel as death, especially since they had hardly anything to eat." This gave rise to general discontent. As Las Casas sagely writes:

> It was inevitable that in the face of so many problems to resolve the Admiral should alienate everyone. To this was added the fact that he was a foreigner and held no fiefs in Castile; he was thus held in little esteem by the Spaniards, especially the highborn, for they have an overweening pride.
>
> [Las Casas, ch. 91.]

A great number of these colonial recruits, led by Fray Buil, returned to Spain the moment that the opportunity to do so presented itself. Columbus had as yet no inkling of this when he decided, in the spring of 1494, to put to sea once again to continue his discoveries. He set sail on April 24, with three caravels specially outfitted for coastal exploration, leaving behind in Hispaniola a governmental council headed by his brother Diego. He was obliged, in fact, to obey the royal instructions enjoining him to explore the islands and mainlands as extensively as possible in order to get there ahead of any expeditions that the King of Portugal might send. And he must not have been at all unhappy to reassume his role of discoverer, to "exercise the appetite and inclination that God had given him and for which He had chosen him." [Las Casas, ch. 94.] His absence was to last five months.

These months of exploration constitute an interlude recalling the atmosphere of the first voyage: we find the same encounters with "noble savages," the same illusions concerning the proximity of Cathay, the same references to the accounts of Marco Polo and Sir John Mandeville.

114

Columbus kept his customary shipboard journal, which he later gave to Andrés Bernáldez, the chaplain of Archdeacon Fonseca. Bernáldez abstracted from it a detailed account which somewhat consoles us for the loss of the original. The journal and other papers were likewise used by Ferdinand Columbus and Las Casas.

Columbus commanded the *Niña*, the caravel that had weathered the great voyage of 1492-1493. The complement of the three ships was made up largely of men from the Andalusian coast, many of whom were glorious veterans of the first exploration of the New World. But there were also Genoese mariners aboard, among them Michele de Cuneo. They also carried several cartographers, one of whom was Juan de la Cosa; a fleet secretary; at least one priest; and an interpreter, the Indian who had been baptised Diego Colón. The company numbered about sixty in all. The Admiral's main objective was to gain further knowledge of Cuba: Was it an island or a mainland? Or was it a promontory of Asia? Putting out to sea on April 24, Columbus set a course straight for the eastern extremity of Cuba (the present-day Cabo Maisí), where he landed without incident. He named it *Cabo Alfa e Omega* to indicate that this was "the end of the Occident and the beginning of the Orient. . . ." From there he ranged the whole long mountainous coast from east to west, keeping the shore close aboard, until he came to its western extremity, to which he gave the name it still bears today, *Cabo de Cruz* – Cape of the Cross – because he had reached it on May 3, the Feast of the True Cross. He then decided to make a detour in the direction of the nearby island of Jamaica, which he took to be Babeque, the site of the much-vaunted gold mines he had heard of long before. "It is the fairest isle that human eyes have ever beheld," he wrote, attempting as usual to conceal his disappointment at not finding a single trace of the precious metal. The Jamaican natives were hostile, moreover, and seemed to be about to throw javelins at the caravels. "To instill a fear of Christians in them," the Admiral ordered a shower of arrows shot at them, and several of the Indians were killed or wounded.

On May 14, Columbus returned to Cabo de Cruz. The

coastline now veered northeast, and the caravels entered a zone of sandy shoals, where navigation was very difficult. Summer had come, and a hurricane broke, accompanied by waterspouts. There now began a period of enormous fatigue and tension for Columbus, and for thirty-two consecutive nights he had almost no sleep. He was elated nonetheless: "He remembered having read," Bernáldez writes, "that according to Sir John Mandeville five thousand islands could be counted in the Indian Sea." Columbus counted as many as 104 islands in this long gulf, to which he gave the lovely name of *Jardín de la Reina* – the Queen's Garden.

The mirages – if such we may call them – grew more and more frequent. "Indians told the Admiral that Magón lay just ahead." [Bernáldez.] Magón was the name of a province of Cuba, but Columbus immediately thought of *Mangi,* Marco Polo's name for South China. "They also said that all the people there have tails, and that was why they wear clothes." The Admiral was not taken in by this story, which he had already heard told of the cannibals; he was, however, much interested in the prospect of meeting people who wore clothes, for this seemed to indicate that he was at last approaching the lands of the Grand Khan.

At approximately the spot where the province of Magón began, they anchored inside a gulf and took a delightful rest along its shores. "Not far inshore two springs of fresh water bubbled forth; they all rested there on the grass amid the scent of flowers, which was wondrous, and the songs of birds." [Bernáldez, from phrases he found in Columbus' journal.]

But not long after, they were terrified:

They entered a sea white as milk. They then found themselves in two fathoms' depth, and there was no hold for their anchors, for once they had dropped them they kept dragging along the bottom. . . . After making ten leagues thus, they were finally able to come to an anchor off an island, in a state of extreme distress.

[Bernáldez, ch. 28.]

The water's white color was caused by a bottom of fine marl that was easily roiled. The waters of this archipelago are still very dangerous to navigate today, even with well-marked charts. What bothered all of them even more was the thought that they had come to the edge of the world – the land's end that Arabic legends described as fringed by interminable shoals. "They would have liked to give up and turn back, but Our Lord, who succors humble men of good will, gave courage unto the Admiral, who decided to go on." [Bernáldez, *ibid.*]

Farther on a strange incident occurred:

> A crossbowman who had gone ashore found himself in the midst of thirty Indians; one of them was wearing a white tunic which reached his feet; the archer thought at first that it was the Trinitarian friar of the ship's company. But two other men clad in white tunics then appeared. He took fright and ran down to the water's edge, crying for help.
>
> [Bernáldez, *ibid.*]

The Spaniards had understood the Indians to say that the mountainous region in the interior was governed by a great king "who they say is holy, and wears a white tunic that reaches the ground." Columbus doubtless thought of Prester John, the priest-potentate whose lands Marco Polo had said lay near the Great Wall of China. Though navigation was extremely difficult, they sailed on in this marshy archipelago until June 8. Columbus' original plan – obviously an unreasonable one – was none other than to circumnavigate the entire globe. On the basis of his wildly erroneous calculations of latitude, he thought he had now sailed around more than half the globe since leaving Spain. In the words of Bernáldez:

> His wish was to find the city of Cathay, in the domain of the Grand Khan ... a province which borders the lands of Prester John. But I told him, when he was my guest in the year 1496, that he would have had to sail at least twelve hundred leagues farther to reach it. ... Had Fortune been with him, he would have attempted to come back to Spain by way of the Orient, the Ganges, and the Arabic Peninsula; and

from there overland to Jerusalem and Jaffa, where he would again have put out to sea.

[Bernáldez, ch. 123.]

But everyone aboard was exhausted, their provisions could not last indefinitely, and the ships were beginning to leak.

On June 12, the Admiral decided to reverse course. He had been ranging the coast of Cuba for more than a month – for Cuba is one of the longest islands in the world – and was not far from its westernmost extremity. But the Indians whom he questioned claimed that one did not reach land's end even after twenty day's journey. Columbus was therefore convinced that this was indeed a promontory of Asia. And there now occurred a famous scene, one which modern minds find incomprehensible: On Columbus' order the Fleet Secretary boards the caravels and "asks the crews if they have any doubt that this land is the terra firma that marks the beginning of the Indies." Out of sheer weariness, no doubt, no one denied the statement. The Secretary then demanded that they sign a deposition attesting to their absolute conviction that they were lying off a continent, "under pain of a fine of 10,000 *maravedis* and having their tongues cut out." [Bernáldez.] The foregoing did not prevent Juan de la Cosa from later representing Cuba as an island! Columbus' personal friend, Michele de Cuneo, also had doubts and submitted them to a "cosmographer" when he returned from Haiti.

Discussing this strange oath, Salvador de Madariaga aptly speaks of "Don Quixotism." Are we not indeed reminded of Don Quixote – "threatening with his lance all those who refused to recognize that Dulcinea was the greatest beauty in all the world"? This is not the only instance, however, in which such an oath was demanded of a ship's crew. When Bartholomeu Dias reversed course after rounding the Cape of Good Hope, he too made his crew swear that it was absolutely fruitless to go on. By acting in this fashion Columbus was hoping to absolve himself of the responsibility of interrupting the exploration which the royal instructions had ordered him to continue.

118

The little fleet therefore turned back. The return passage was arduous, but it was marked by two picturesque and touching episodes. According to Bernáldez' account:

One Sunday the Admiral ordered mass to be said in a spot full of thistles in flower, which were more fragrant than orange-blossoms. When the cacique of the region saw the boat touch shore, he took the Admiral by the hand, and an old Indian more than eighty years old took his other hand; this latter was holding a basket of apples, which he offered as a gift. . . . Holding each other thus by the hands, and escorted by a great crowd of Indians, they arrived at the place that had been readied for the mass. When the Admiral had finished praying, the old Indian bravely addressed him, telling him not to be lifted up by pride, for like all other men he too was mortal, that all men were born naked and had an immortal soul, and that after their death the soul either ascended to Heaven or descended into Hell, according to whether it had acted well or badly. The Admiral was pleased to hear this, and understood almost all of it, thanks to the gestures the old man made. He answered him, through his Indian interpreter, saying that he had come to do no harm, save to the wicked, and that he had already much honored the righteous, following in this the express will of his rulers, the King and Queen of Castile. "Do you mean to say, then," the old man retorted, addressing the interpreter, "that this Admiral obeys another ruler?" "Yes," the Indian said, "he obeys the King and Queen of Castile, who are the greatest sovereigns in the world." And then he told him, and all the Indians present, of the marvels that he had seen in Spain: cities, fortresses, horses, fiestas, tourneys, bull-fights. They listened with great delight, and the story passed from one to the other. The old man declared that he would like to see such things, and would willingly have accompanied the Admiral to Spain, had not his wife and son protested, weeping.

[Bernáldez, ch. 30.]

The other encounter with "noble savages" took place in Jamaica – for Columbus had decided to finish exploring this island, sailing this time along the south coast, where the natives proved very hospitable. The caravels were just about to leave when three dugout canoes came out to meet them. In the words of Bernáldez:

In the largest canoe were the cacique, his wife, his two daughters – one of whom was about eighteen years of age and most beautiful – naked, as was their custom, but most modest; his two sons, his five brothers, and others of his retinue. In the bow of the canoe stood a man dressed as a herald. He wore a cloak of colored plumes shaped like a coat of mail, on his head was a coronet of plumes, and in his hand he held a white banner. . . . The cacique wore on his breast jewels of a sort of copper they call *guanin*, which looks like gold; he wore an ornament on his forehead, and gold disks in his ears. Although he was otherwise completely naked, he wore a girdle of colored stones. . . . When the canoe reached the ship the cacique began to distribute native handiwork to the crew. It was morning; the Admiral was at his prayers and did not notice the arrival of this cacique. The latter came aboard the caravel with all his retinue, and as soon as he caught sight of the Admiral, went up to him with joyful mien, and addressed these words to him: "Friend, I am determined to quit my country and go with you to your rulers, who are the greatest sovereigns in the world, because it is at their command that you march through our lands, bringing them beneath your yoke, as I have learned from your Indians, and because even the great Carib tribe fears you since you destroyed their canoes and took their sons prisoner. For this reason, before you take my lands and domains from me, I wish to board your ships, taking my retinue with me, so that I may go look upon the great King and the great Queen and see the marvels of Castile, which your Indian tells me are beyond number." But the Admiral took pity on him, his daughters, his sons, his wife. He answered him saying that he would receive him as a vassal of the King and Queen of Spain, but

*Indians being driven into slavery. (Théodore de Bry, Americae pars IV).*

that he could not take him along at that time; that he would satisfy his desire another time. They took their leave of each other as do good friends.

[Bernáldez, ch. 131.]

After having explored the south coast of Haiti Columbus finally returned to Isabela on September 29, 1494. He was ill when he arrived: ". . . having been seized by a pestilential torpor . . . he suddenly lost all his strength and it was thought that he would not live through another day." [Las Casas, ch. 99.] He recovered, but had to take to his bed for several months, suffering from another painful attack of arthritis.

Years of great tribulation were about to begin for the Governor-Viceroy. A valuable aide, it is true, awaited him: his brother Bartholomew, who had gone from

*Collecting gold. (Théodore de Bry, Americae pars VI).*

France to Spain, and from there to the "Indies." But Bartholomew had had no more success than Diego in governing the Spanish colonists, who had scattered all over the island prospecting for gold. Since they had extorted the most reprehensible tributes, the Indians' reaction had taken the form of ambushes and assassinations. There then began a ghastly vicious circle of reprisals. Columbus sent several military expeditions into the interior. There were pitched battles, and naturally the victory fell to the Christians. This, then, was the situation in the Vega Real in the spring of 1495. More than five hundred captives were taken and shipped off to Spain to be sold as slaves. Naturally Las Casas bitterly criticized this cruel conduct on the part of the Admiral, which he believed was motivated by the colony's financial difficulties: "He sanctioned enslavement of the Indians in order to give the lie to those who criticized the affair of the Indies, saying that the expenses there were many and the profits null." [Las Casas, I, 107.]

After the capture of the valiant cacique Caonabó by Captain Hojeda, pacification of the island was relatively successful. But the Viceroy was still obliged to justify the enormous expenses of the colony: there were salaries to pay, and supply-lines to set up (for the hidalgos refused to work.) He conceived the idea of exacting a gold tribute from the new Spanish "subjects," but the amount levied was too great and forced the Indians to the exhausting labor of sluicing sand and gold-bearing gravel. Many of them fell ill from it and took refuge in the mountains.

During the summer of 1495 the long-coveted gold mine of Cibao was finally discovered, not far from Santo Tomás. Columbus entrusted the task of exploiting the mine to his brother Bartholomew (whom he had previously appointed *Adelantado* – Lieutenant General). "They found there," Peter Martyr writes in his *Second Decade,* "shafts that had been dug long before. The Admiral thought that he had found in these mines the ancient treasures of King Solomon. It is not my task to decide whether this be true or false." Columbus was to argue in the affirmative all the rest of his life, writing on several occasions: "Hispaniola, that is to say Ophir. . . ." He ordered a fortress built near the mine, and named it *Concepción* in honor of the Virgin, placing it beneath the protection of a great cross erected on the top. This cross was said to be miraculous. (Twenty years later Oviedo recorded a tradition that he had heard in the island: a skirmish with the Indians had taken place, during which they had seized the cross; but they were unable to set fire to it, and fled in terror.)

Despite the wars and his financial difficulties Columbus had not completely lost sight of his primary aim, the conversion of the Indians, for during this year – 1495 – the Viceroy took the time to draw up a sort of ethnographic memorandum on the religion of the natives. This report was copied by Ferdinand Columbus in his *History:*

I have not been able to detect any sort of idolatry among the Indians, nor any religious sect. Each of their kings, however, has a dwelling-place apart from the village, in which are found carved wooden images, that they call *cemíes*. Certain ceremonies are held therein, as is done in our churches; they put powders in the heads of the statues, then inhale thereof through a reed and lose their senses in the manner of drunken men. These statues represent, so far as I can see, their father or ancestor or predecessor. They venerate some of these more or less than others, as we do our statues carried in processions.... Most of them show great devotion for three sorts of stones: the first is said to favor harvests, the second women in childbirth, the third rain and sun.... I have taken great pains to learn what their beliefs are concerning the abode of the dead, having questioned Caonabó in particular [Caonabó was Columbus' prisoner], the grand cacique of this island, a mature man who is most knowledgeable and sharp-witted. He and others tell me that the dead go to a certain valley where they rejoin their ancestors, that there they eat and take wives and divert themselves most pleasantly, as can be seen below in the account of Fray Ramón Pane, whom I enjoined to learn their language and record all their rites and antiquities. It may thus be concluded that the Indians have a certain natural belief in the immortality of the soul.

Though the other monks had sailed off with Fray Buil, Ramón Pane had stayed behind in the island, where – with Columbus' encouragement – he had proved himself a fine missionary. The "ethnographic" report he drew up was published by Ferdinand Columbus and utilized by Peter Martyr. In it we follow his establishment of successive missionary stations, first at the fort of Magdalena (where he succeeded in converting a cacique and his brother, who were to prove faithful to the point of martyrdom), then at the fort of Concepción, where for two years he catechized the cacique Guarionex (who became an apostate when he saw that the Christians were cruel, and seized his lands). Among the "antiquities" recorded by Fray Pane was this striking native prophecy:

"There will come men wearing clothes, who will dominate us and kill us." "They had originally believed," the monk adds, "that this oracular revelation concerned the cannibals. They now think that it means the Admiral and his company."

A letter of this same year – 1495 – addressed to the "Admiral of the Indies in the great isle of Cibao," compared Columbus to a true apostle. The author of this letter was Jaime Ferrer, a Catalan cosmographer and dealer in precious stones who had known the discoverer in Barcelona in the days of his great triumph. Having been consulted by the Sovereigns at the time of the Treaty of Tordesillas, Ferrer had furnished them a world-map and advised them how to calculate marine leagues, deferring to the authority of the "Great Admiral of the Indies who knows more of this than any other man and whom Divine Providence has chosen, on account of this great mystery, to make His Glory manifest." It is important to note the terms that Ferrer uses to address this Elect of God:

> ... Soon, Sire, you will be in the Sinus Magnus [the Gulf of Bengal] near that land which is the last resting-place of Saint Thomas; soon there shall be fulfilled that which Supreme Truth has declared: the whole world shall come under one Shepherd and one Law; this shall come to be only if these peoples, more naked in doctrine than in body, are taught our Holy Faith. I thus believe I make no mistake, Sire, in affirming that you are fulfilling the office of apostle and ambassador of God, chosen to reveal His Name to lands still ignorant of Truth. It would not be amiss for one of the Cardinals of Rome – in the manner of an apostle – to take part in your glorious mission; but the weight of their great capes and the laxity of their way of life hinder this. ... If your soul be at times lifted up to contemplate the glorious office incumbent upon you, let it loudly proclaim, to the sound of the harp: *Non nobis, Domine, sed Nomini Tuo da gloriam* [Not our name, O Lord, but Thine be glorified].

An elegantly subtle allusion is made to the difficulties encountered by the Admiral:

Forasmuch, Sire, as you have tasted, in the course of your pilgrimage more divine than human, of the savor of bitterness that tinges Holy Bread taken in the service of the Creator, you know beyond all doubt that in this world temporal fame and eternal glory are not won by idleness.

Columbus' reputation at court had indeed suffered. Even if the Sovereigns made allowance for the disappointment of those who had returned from the Indies empty-handed – not having succeeded in "gathering in gold by the shovelful" – they could hardly fail to heed the complaints of a churchman such as Fray Buil, who accused the Governor of highhandedness in the distribution of supplies. The arrival in Seville of the hapless Indian prisoners (whose numbers had been decimated, moreover, by the rough crossing) had also produced a bad impression. Overcome by scruples, Their Majesties had assembled a commission of theologians to determine whether they had the right to put them up for sale.

As a consequence the supply ships which departed for the Indies in the summer of 1495 had among their complement a Royal Commissioner, Juan Aguado. This was a great humiliation for the Viceroy, but he nonetheless gave the appearance of complying cheerfully. Aguado had not been sent to censure him openly, but Columbus was quite aware that this represented a fall from favor. Worse still, discontent was spreading all about him. "The favorite oath of all the colonists was: 'I swear it, as God may take me back to Castile!'" [Las Casas, ch. 108.] The Viceroy would doubtless have returned immediately to the mother country to present his governor's report, had not a storm destroyed a number of ships in the poorly protected harbor of Isabela. According to Oviedo and Las Casas, it was at this juncture that he began to wear the habit of a Franciscan friar – a robe of coarse wool girdled about the waist with a cord – and allowed his beard to grow. Since he was a simple lay-friar of the Third Order of Saint Francis, this was in no wise obligatory; he adopted this habit out of penitence, either because of the disaster that had occurred to his ships, or as a sort of ostentatious show of humility at a time that seemed to him a threatening portent of things to come.

On March 10, 1496, Columbus set sail for Spain, having delegated his administrative powers to his brother Bartholomew and his judicial powers to an equerry of his household named Francisco Roldán, who was to have the title of *Alcalde Mayor* – Chief Justice.

The long crossing, full of incidents, ended with the debarkation at Cádiz. They entered the city of Seville in splendid ceremonial procession; the Admiral's cortege again included Indians, but this time the Genoese was clad in the humble habit of Saint Francis. He accepted the hospitality of the curate Andrés Bernáldez, gave him an account of his adventures, and told him of the rancors he had provoked "because he did not let his men profiteer, being ever careful to preserve that due the Royal Treasury." Shortly thereafter he was summoned to Burgos by the Sovereigns, and there received a most cordial welcome, for Aguado had been unable to report a single valid reason for censuring Columbus. He presented his Indians: a brother and a nephew of Caonabó, bearing masks, girdles, collars, and the magnificent crown of the great cacique. "All these jewels," Bernáldez writes, "bore the figure of the Devil, in the form of an owl or a cat's head." The sovereigns showed themselves well pleased on all counts, and were most interested in the report of the lands that had been discovered. But jealousy on the part of the royal entourage was not dissipated, for the accounts of many of the repatriated colonists had played a large part in discrediting the settlement at Hispaniola. The Admiral was later to write:

> I reported to Your Majesties on the peoples I had visited, and the means by which their souls could be saved; I told them of the tributes from the inhabitants of Hispaniola, who hold you as their suzerains; I displayed gold nuggets in great number, spoke of the gold mines, presented many specimens of spices. All that was ill-received by certain persons full of envy and malice, for they could not bear that I should speak of the service of Our Lord, and that I should point out how greatly this honored Your Majesties.

127

I explained, indeed, that tribulations and expenditures had both a temporal and a spiritual end; that it was impossible that in time Spain should not realize great profit therefrom. I recounted what great princes had done to add to their renown: thus Solomon, who sent his ships to the farthest point of the Orient to reconnoiter the mountain of Ophir (and Hispaniola is that very mountain); or Alexander, who ordered the isle of Taprobane in the Indies to be explored; or Nero, who sent expeditions to the headwaters of the Nile.... To return to our own era, I spoke of the Sovereigns of Portugal and the constancy of purpose they have evidenced in the discovery of Guinea, of the money and men they have expended therein, perhaps as many as half the population of Portugal, yet they persevered. ... All that I said did naught but feed the scorn and neglect shown my undertaking. But Your Majesties answered me with a smile, saying that I should take no account thereof. One day when I was apprising them of my fears (for the calumnies being spread against me might at last have had effect on them, as water falling drop by drop upon a stone comes with time to pierce it through), they answered me, with that magnanimity for which the world esteems them, saying that I should in no wise be aggrieved: though nothing should ever be found there save stones and trees, they would pursue this undertaking ... for they considered that our Holy Faith would have greater dominion thereby.

Despite these royal assurances, how far Columbus was from forgetting his concern for the profits to be gained from Hispaniola! If only he had been truly convinced of the primacy of the spiritual purpose in whose name he spoke so eloquently; if only he had abandoned his policy of enslavement! He did no such thing, and salved the conscience of the Sovereigns in this regard by explaining that the Indians sent to Spain had been captured in "just wars," in reprisal for the crimes they had committed against the Christians. And Bartholomew received permission to load three ships with this human cattle. . . . Las Casas duly stigmatizes this aberration of the Admiral (the origin of which he considers to be the slave trade policies of the Portuguese, which Columbus had witnessed in Guinea):

> Should he not have placed love for his neighbor above the wish to gain money for the Sovereigns; should he not have envisaged the true aim of the Discovery, the salvation of all these souls, instead of using force and violence, bringing ignominy to the very name of Christian?
>
> [Las Casas, ch. 106.]

The case could not be better stated. . . .

Columbus was to remain in Spain for two years before again putting out to sea. These two years no doubt seemed endless to this impatient man whose imagination was never at rest. Very frequently he stayed at court, in the company of his two sons who were now in the service of the Infante as pages. But the affair of the Indies was not the foremost concern of the Sovereigns, who were busy strengthening the position of the royal house through anti-French alliances; two of their children were to marry members of the House of Burgundy: the Infanta Juana (who was later to be called Juana la Loca – the Mad) left for Flanders in the month of August, 1496, to marry the Archduke Philip the Fair of Austria; the same fleet of 120 ships that had escorted her there brought back the Archduchess Margaret (Philip's sister), who was betrothed to the heir of the throne of Castile. The marriage took place at Burgos, on April 3, 1497, and Columbus was present at the ceremony. Soon afterward he obtained a number of royal ordinances (dated Burgos, April 23, and the months that followed) concerning either his personal privileges or his future departure for the Indies.

Let us stop to examine the first of these documents. It is another royal confirmation (the fifth since 1492) of the *Capitulations* of Santa-Fé, the basic document establishing the rights of Columbus. One addition was made: Columbus obtained permission to establish a *mayorazgo,* or entail, settling his estate on his descend-

ants, "in order that your memory may be perpetuated."
The entailment was executed by the Admiral some months
later, in February of 1498. Under the pretext that the
original of this document has not come down to us,
certain hypercritical scholars have called it a forgery:
their motive (whether it be openly avowed or not) lies in
the fact that in this document there occurs the famous
phrase concerning "Genoa, the city where I was born."
(Salvador de Madariaga, who refuses to recognize Columbus' love for Genoa, stands with those who believe it a
forgery.) But in 1925 there was discovered, in the
archives of Simancas, a royal confirmation of this entailment, dated 1501; it is difficult to believe that between
1498 and 1501 a forged document was fabricated to fit
the needs of a lawsuit involving the estate that took
place as late as 1566, as Luis Ulloa would have it. The
very idea of establishing this fief, to be inherited by
primogeniture, and of having it confirmed some years
later, is quite consistent with what we know of Columbus.[1]

The principal provisions of the entail were as follows:
"Since we are all mortal . . . it seemed to me proper that
I should establish an entail from the income from the
eighth of the profits granted me." Christopher's heir was
to be his elder son Diego, or in the event of Diego's
death, his younger son Ferdinand. (In the event of Ferdinand's death, Bartholomew, Christopher's brother, would
succeed; then Diego, his other brother.) The heir was
enjoined to adopt as his signature his monogram alone,
followed by one title only: The Admiral; to provide an
income in Genoa for "a member of our family, who is
to live there and take a wife there, for it is from this
city that I came originally; to purchase shares in the
Bank of San Giorgio in Genoa and add to what these
brought in the sum necessary "to do some pious deed in
regard to Jerusalem . . . for at the time that I resolved
to sail off to discover the Indies, I begged Their Majesties

---

[1]   Charles Verlinden (in *Studi Colombiani*, II; Genoa, 1952) points
out that it is this same backward-looking "medieval and feudal"
preoccupation which in 1497 made Columbus insist on modeling
his privileges as Admiral of the Ocean Sea on the privileges of
Admirals of Castile.

to use all the profit that should come therefrom for the conquest of Jerusalem." Diego was to make every effort to participate in this crusade personally; to put all his resources at the disposition of the Holy Church in the event of schisms or heresies; to construct in Hispaniola a church dedicated to the Conception of the Virgin, and a hospital; to endow four chairs there for professors of theology, who were to devote themselves to ccnversion of the Indians, or even more than four, if the revenues from the entail should increase, "for to this end it is well to spend all that one can."

A large number of royal ordinances gave instructions, complete to the last detail, for the voyage that the Admiral was preparing to undertake. He was to outfit six ships at the Crown's expense. "You are to select 333 persons, *viz.*: 40 gentlemen volunteers, 100 foot soldiers, 30 able seamen, 30 ship's boys, 20 gold-sluicers, 50 day laborers, 20 artisans of various sorts, 30 women" (this last was an important innovation, for a great part of the hatred aroused by the Spaniards had stemmed from the fact that they had carried off Indian women with no scruples whatsoever). "You will take to the Indies a number of monks and ecclesiastics who are men of virtue, in order that they may administer the sacraments [to the Spaniards] and attempt to convert the Indians to our Holy Faith. . . . You will also take a physician, an apothecary, an herbalist, and musical instruments for the diversion of those who there establish themselves." One provision allowed the recruiting of petty criminals as future colonists – and this was done. The Admiral was to be responsible for distributing plots of land among the new settlers. (He himself refused a fief in Hispaniola that the Sovereigns offered him.) The spiritual aim of colonization was again defined: "Above all, as soon as you arrive in the aforementioned islands, you will attempt to lead the said Indians to live in peace."

The greatest problem was to raise funds. The Royal Treasury had been exhausted by the marriages of the royal offspring, and a third marriage was celebrated in the autumn of 1497: that of the Infanta Isabella and the new King of Portugal, Dom Manuel; this was an important union, for it ended the rivalry between the two sister countries. There was also a war to be waged against France for possession of Rousillon.

The Viceroy's personal accounts with the Sovereigns were hard to settle. In previous years Columbus had advanced money to pay the salaries of officials in Hispaniola; this was reimbursed. To undertake the new expedition the Royal Treasury had allotted him a large sum, but six months later he had received only an eighth of it and again had to resort to loans from Italian bankers.

The objective assigned the expedition was not only the maintenance of the existing colony of Hispaniola, but also an exploration farther to the south, where because of what his Indian informants had told him Columbus had high hopes of discovering vast expanses of land: if these were discovered to the east of the line of demarcation, they would belong to Portugal, but this no longer presented any difficulty.

During the winter of 1497-1498 Columbus made the acquaintance of a man who was to be one of his most faithful friends: Fray Gaspar Gorricio (a native of the North of Italy), a monk from the celebrated Carthusian monastery of Las Cuevas on the banks of the Guadalquivir on the outskirts of Seville. (Columbus was later to be buried in the monastery chapel, and his son Ferdinand was to build a magnificent residence nearby.) Columbus found in Gorricio at once a spiritual advisor, an archivist, and a treasurer.

The Captain-General of the future armada now gave his orders: of the six ships three were to provision the colony; the command of one of them was entrusted to Pedro de Harana, the brother of Beatriz Enríquez; another was to be captained by Giovanni Antonio Colombo, a Genoese cousin of Christopher's.

But the preparations dragged on at the Council for the Affair of the Indies, and the Admiral suspected ill-will on the part of Fonseca. "I was on the point of abandoning everything," he later wrote. A veritable catastrophe had just occurred: the totally unexpected death, on November 6, 1497, of the Infante Juan, only shortly after his marriage. This was a terrible shock to Queen Isabella, who was a devoted mother. Columbus, who was on intimate terms with the royal family (he had already been a party to the Queen's anxieties when a storm had delayed the arrival of the Infante's betrothed), maintained – exaggerating, no doubt, as was his habit – that only the prospect of his new voyage to the Indies could turn the Queen's thoughts from her bereavement: ". . . and, to lighten her burden of sorrow what little I could, I undertook this new expedition."

The Admiral grew more and more exasperated during his stay in Seville. His impatience was quite legitimate, moreover, for he had a presentiment that his brother Bartholomew, whom he had left behind in Hispaniola as Lieutenant Governor, was in the midst of grave difficulties. Under these circumstances, he grew less and less able to bear the mocking jokes that were making the rounds about *his* affair of the Indies, and the delays brought about by administrative red tape. One of the Royal Commissioners, Ximeno de Breviesca, drew attention to himself by making remarks that were particularly insolent, and Columbus was bitterly offended. His violent rancor suddenly exploded the very day that everything was ready at last, on May 30, 1498, to put out to sea: "The aforementioned Ximeno, who was not an Old Christian, had wandered up onto the quarterdeck of the flagship. The Admiral threw himself upon him, kicking him roundly, tearing out his hair, and putting him in a sad state." This brutal behavior was totally unexpected on the part of so sober a man as Columbus, and in the opinion of Las Casas, who reports the incident, it made a most unfavorable impression on the Sovereigns. Columbus was later to write, with few apologies:

I beg Your Majesties to choose officials for the Affair of the Indies from among those men who are not opposed to it. Speaking of this, I do not know what has become of Ximeno; but he belongs to the race of those who ever come to each other's aid, whether it be to die or to live.

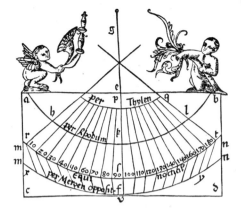

# THE THIRD VOYAGE

Las Casas and Ferdinand, in their own accounts, reproduce the substance of Columbus' shipboard journal, which has disappeared. We also have some knowledge of the letters that Columbus sent to Their Catholic Majesties, thanks to the long extracts from them cited by Las Casas.

The six vessels set sail on May 30, 1498, "in the name of the Holy Trinity," as was their custom. Once they had reached the Canaries, the Admiral detached three of the ships, which were to sail directly to Hispaniola. The other three sailed down to the Cape Verde Islands, where they put into port, and then sailed on farther to the latitude of Sierra Leone, the region where the Portuguese were finding gold. Like the "men of erudition" of his time, Columbus believed that regions lying on the same parallel had the same type of inhabitants and produced the same materials; thus (as his friend Jaime Ferrer had insisted) the hotter a region was, the more precious products it contained.

Having arrived at this latitude, the Admiral therefore set a southwesterly course on July 4. He writes:

> May He who is One and Three guide me in His goodness and mercy, in order that I may bring Their

135

*Saint Christopher (undoubtedly an allusion to Columbus), with the isthmus of Panama in the background.*
*(Chart of Juan de la Cosa, 1500. Museo Naval, Madrid).*

Majesties and all Christendom great joy, as happened when I discovered the Indies, an event the whole world has heard of.

The existence of the continent of South America and the fact that it stretched far to the east were apparently suspected by the Portuguese. "I wish to verify," Columbus continues, "what Dom João claims, namely that there is a very large mainland toward the west" (and it was no doubt for this reason that John II in 1494 had asked that the line be moved farther west). The Admiral had also heard reports from the Indians of Haiti that "black people" had come there from a place far to the south of the islands, bringing with them a metal called *guanin* (an alloy of gold and copper).

On July 13, the vessels entered the doldrums, a belt of calms so hot that the water butts and wine casks burst, and lard and salt meat spoiled. The Admiral was worn out from worry and insomnia. But "with God's aid," the wind freshened, pushing them westward; on July 31, land was sighted: it was an island (close to the shore of what is now Venezuela). Since the profile of three summits was visible, Columbus saw in this a "sign" and gave it the name of *Trinidad,* which it still bears. After the indispensable trip ashore to take on fresh water, the Admiral sailed around the island and into the Gulf of Paria: on August 1, he sighted the American continent for the first time, but took it to be an island and named it *Isla Santa* – Blessed Isle. The most amazing surprises awaited him in this gulf, the like of which he had never seen, and which he finally decided was the mouth of one of the rivers of the Terrestrial Paradise! He found himself in a sort of inland freshwater sea, imprisoned between the many mouths of the Orinoco delta and the islands of Trinidad, yet leading to the ocean through two narrow channels. The first surprise: the natives were not black, as Columbus expected; they looked like other Indians, "but whiter in color, tall in stature, with long straight hair." A cacique from the island of Trinidad "wearing a golden diadem approached the Admiral, who was wearing a crimson cap, bowed to him, then took

136

off his cap and put the diadem in its place." On August 4, the ships nearly foundered in an enormous tidal wave in the narrow south channel (which Columbus named *Boca de la Sierpe* – the Serpent's Mouth – no doubt an allusion to the Devil). Columbus later wrote:

> Late at night, while I was standing on the quarter-deck, I heard a terrible din. I saw the sea rise up in the form of a gigantic swell as high as the ship, and roll slowly down upon us. The crest of the wave produced a furious roaring noise; even today I can still feel my body tremble with fright.

The ships were not swamped, however, and finally managed to drop anchor on the north coast of the gulf, on the peninsula of Paria, a promontory so long that Columbus took it for an island and attempted to sail westward around it.

Because he was suffering from inflamed eyes, he was unable to go ashore to preside over the customary possession ceremony. After a week of exploration along the low verdant coast he decided to turn back, though he was enormously intrigued by this immense fresh-water gulf, at the other end of which a boat-party sent to reconnoiter had found the four mouths of a river (the Orinoco). Las Casas writes:

> He would have indeed liked to penetrate the secret of these lands, discover whence came the gold and pearls [that the Indians wore]. But he feared that the provisions he was carrying for the colonists of Hispaniola – an affair that had cost him much trouble – might spoil, and he therefore decided to return there, being free thereafter to dispatch his brother, the Adelantado, forthwith to pursue the discovery.
>
> [Las Casas, ch. 137.]

On August 12, he found himself in the narrow channel leading from the gulf to the open sea. They arrived there at the hour of tierce, just as the fresh water of the gulf and the salt water of the sea met in roaring tide rips, and a great swell as high as a mountain rose amid a mighty

137

din; as had happened once before in the Boca de la Sierpe, they were sure they were about to perish, but the gulf current carried them safely out to sea. The Admiral cried out that they had escaped the "dragon's mouth" (as in one of the Psalms), whence the name *Boca del Drago*, which this dangerous strait still bears.

Suffering increasing pain in his eyes, Columbus gave up exploring the coast of Venezuela – where he would eventually have come upon pearl-fisheries – then set a northwesterly course, and on August 31, dropped anchor off Santo Domingo, on the south coast of Haiti.

Before going ashore Columbus finished writing a long letter to the Sovereigns, accompanied by a navigation chart; this is an enormously interesting letter, for it gives us a firsthand view of his effort to reconcile what he has just observed in these newly discovered lands with the theoretical and theological knowledge he already possessed.

His basic ideas of what the world was like came from charts in Ptolemy's *Geography* (though as we have seen he followed the calculations of Marinus of Tyre and thus thought that Asia stretched even farther eastward). Since the time of Ptolemy, navigation charts had shown no territory farther east than a place referred to as *Cattigara* (the west coast of the Indo-Chinese Peninsula). Maps of Asia stopped there, and farther to the south a long arc of a circle was drawn, linking Asia and South Africa, and bearing the legend *Terra Incognita* – Unknown Land. Columbus believed that he had entered these environs: in this letter he says very clearly that he has discovered "a new hemisphere, unknown to the ancients." This is an important statement, for it is not too different from the one for which Amerigo Vespucci is renowned: "Ptolemy and other sages who described the world said that it was spherical, like the hemisphere in which they lived. . . . But there is another half of the world of which they had no knowledge." For various reasons Columbus imagined that this hemisphere was pear-shaped: its temperature was milder than that found in the same latitude in African waters; the natives were much lighter in color than those in Africa. Thus altitude probably served to correct the effect of latitude. He writes:

138

I am therefore persuaded that this hemisphere is not round – that is to say the one beginning beyond the place where the Indies fall off into the ocean [i.e., the southern hermisphere], the extremity of which lies beneath the equator; furthermore, Aristotle says that the Antarctic pole is the highest part of the world, and lies closest to the sky. . . . No one as yet had any clear notion of this hemisphere, for no one had ever come here until now, when Your Majesties sent me to explore it.

A second hypothesis, complementary to the first, now occurred to him: this region might lie close to the Terrestrial Paradise. From the beginnings of the Christian era, Church authors had frequently maintained that the Garden of Eden was still to be found on our globe. In descriptions of the world (among them the *Imago mundi,* one of Columbus' favorite books) and even on maps, an exact location of Paradise was indicated, usually at the remotest point in the Far East, on a high mountain that the waters of the Flood had not inundated, in a hot region just a little south of the equator; it was represented as having four great rivers flowing through it. Columbus believed that he had arrived at this far point of the Orient. But because the coast that he found there was flat, Paradise could not be in the immediate vicinity. He writes:

. . . but I do not believe that it is a steep mountain, as is usually written; the earth must rise gradually, beginning in regions far from here. I do not believe, moreover, that any person can reach Paradise, unless it be through the express will of God. This river probably flows down from the summit and comes to form a sort of lake [the Gulf of Paria], for I have never heard tell of such a great quantity of fresh water meeting salt water. . . . This moderate temperature is still another sign of Paradise.

There follows a passage in which he glimpses the truth:

If this river does not flow from out of Paradise,

139

it comes from an immense land to the south, whereof no one until now has had any knowledge.

And he now turns back to the "authorities" he had cited before his first voyage to prove that the world contained more dry land than oceans: Aristotle, Seneca, Pliny, Cardinal d'Ailly, the "prophet" Esdras (to whom he had since added Petrus Comestor – the master of scholastic History – and Francisco de Mayrones):

> If this be a *terra firma,* it is a most amazing thing, and will be considered such by all scholars, since the river that empties herein is so large that there is fresh water as far as 48 leagues out to sea.

He then adds (and this does not contradict his intuition that this is a continent):

> But I am convinced that the Terrestrial Paradise lies yonder, and I shall forthwith send my brother, the Adelantado, to go farther inland in these regions.

This "pro-Paradise" conclusion is obviously false, but to Columbus it seemed further confirmed by a piece of evidence he had seen with his own eyes: when they left the Gulf of Paria his ships were suddenly driven on by a violent current although there was no wind. (This is a well-known phenomenon today, and is caused by the equatorial current which runs from west to east.) To Columbus is seemed easily explainable on the ground that they were descending the slope of the Terrestrial Paradise!

Let us not laugh at all this too hastily. So long as the earth was considered to be the center of the universe, religious faith was shackled to a whole series of cosmogonic conceptions. And as late as the middle of the sixteenth century there was a tendency to consider those who denied the existence of the Terrestrial Paradise on our globe as heretical.[1]

---

[1] See Dom Anselme Stolz: *Théologie de la mystique,* Chevetogne, 1939.

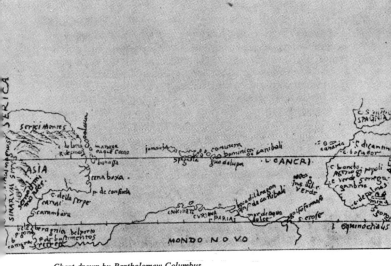

*Chart drawn by Bartholomew Columbus
(1503), showing the "Mondo Novo" — the New World. (Biblioteca di Firenze).*

Though it was not yet fully understood, the intuition that *another world* had been discovered dates from this voyage of Columbus: not the *new world* of the West Indies – so named by Peter Martyr – but *another world* in the true sense, a world unknown even to the ancients. This does not mean, naturally, that Columbus realized that South America was a continent separated from Asia by a vast ocean; he imagined his "terra firma" to lie quite close to the "Indies," and doubtless believed that is was situated in somewhat the same position that Australia occupies in relation to Asia. A chart of 1503 ascribed to Bartholomew Columbus gives the name *New World* to that part of the South American continent that had been discovered up to that date. This chart is probably a copy of the chart of the third voyage drawn up by the Admiral, but the latter document has unfortunately been lost.

141

Other explorers promptly set sail in the Admiral's track as soon as his report reached Spain, and profited from the information indicated on his chart. The most important of these voyages was that of Alonso de Hojeda, who had sailed with Columbus on the second voyage; accompanied by Juan de la Cosa and the Florentine Amerigo Vespucci, he explored a large region on the coasts of Venezuela and found the pearl-fisheries that Columbus had had to omit from his itinerary.

Two terrible years were about to begin for the unfortunate Viceroy. Arriving at Hispaniola, he rejoined his two brothers, Bartholomew and Diego, who had settled in Santo Domingo, the new capital. (It had been founded by Bartholomew, who had given it this name in memory of their father, Domenico Columbus.) Columbus found himself confronted with a revolution in the making: Francisco Roldán, whom he had appointed to the post of *Alcalde Mayor* – Chief Justice – before he left, had not been able to bear being made accountable to a foreigner in the person of Bartholomew, who as Adelantado enjoyed complete control over the island; hoping perhaps that these Genoese would be repudiated and replaced following the report of Aguado, the Royal Commissioner, Roldán had seceded with about seventy of the colonists, "pointing out to them that they would be able to act as they pleased, would no longer have to work, and would have plenty to eat and many women." [Letter from Columbus to the Sovereigns.] Roldán had at the same time pacified the cacique of the province of Xaragua, where he had settled, by exempting the Indians from paying the gold-tribute they found so onerous. In other provinces of the island the caciques had rebelled against the Adelantado, in order that they too might be exempted from the tribute. In the course of several armed encounters many Indians had been captured, and at the very moment that Columbus arrived in Santo Domingo, three caravels were in the roadstead, loaded with slaves and ready to return to Spain. The number of those who had remained loyal was not large, and included quite a few malcontents and disease-ridden colonists (syphilis had now made its appearance in the New World).

The Viceroy's attitude toward the rebels was to show a disconcerting lack of firmness: this doubtless stemmed from his fatigue, and from an inferiority complex as well, for he sensed that his reputation had suffered, and that the affair of the Indies no longer enjoyed the total support of the Crown. He wrote Roldán a letter whose tone was almost cordial, sent him a safe-conduct to come to Santo Domingo, and gave his permission to any malcontents who so chose to return to Spain aboard the caravels that were about to set sail. This they did.

The messages that Columbus addressed to the Court on October 18 were of two sorts. On the one hand, he sent an account of the exciting exploration along the borders of the "Terrestrial Paradise," together with a chart, specimens of gold, and a hundred or so pearls which the natives of Paria had given him. He also dispatched, on the other hand, a long letter concerning the situation in Hispaniola. Its first point: since the ships had already been loaded with Indians, the Viceroy once again emphasized the profit that could be made from them:

> It is the custom to use many black slaves in Castile, in Aragon, in Portugal, in Italy, in Sicily, in the Canary Islands, and I am quite sure that not as many are being shipped from Guinea as before; now a single one of these Indians is well worth three Blacks. I found myself in the Cape Verde Islands [at the beginning of this voyage of exploration] where there is a busy trade in slaves, and I saw that they were going for a price of 8,000 *maravedis*. . . . From these two products [slaves and "brazil-wood"] it seems to me that one could make a profit of 40 million *maravedis,* so long as there is no lack of ships to sail here. . . . Although the Indians perish at present, this will not always be the case, for this is what happened to the Blacks and the Canary Islanders at first.

A more open espousal of the slave trade would be hard to imagine! Let us here repeat Las Casas' commentary on the subject:

> It is beyond all belief that a man whom I can call

143

naught but good and well-intentioned should prove so blind in regard to so clear an issue. One might answer me by saying that this is not so strange, since so many learned men in the Sovereigns' entourage proved equally blind, and sanctioned the custom of gaining worldly profit from cargoes of innocent Indians who were treated like mere heads of cattle!

We find what seems to be a trace of remorse in a letter written by Columbus shortly before his death:

> When I sent a great number of Indians to Castile to be sold, I intended that they be given instruction in Our Faith and customs, and then be sent back to their homeland so that they might teach the others.

Let us now go back to the Viceroy's epistle. Assuming a mode of expression that will subsequently occur more and more frequently in his writings, he hides his fear of the Sovereigns' disapproval beneath religious considerations and a reminder of the calumny he is having to endure:

> I have ever had to combat the Enemy of our Holy Faith, for he has worked with all his might to demolish my great undertaking.... But God is the creator thereof, and He will bring it to fulfillment as He has done since the beginning.... Let those who have read the histories of the Greeks and Romans give answer unto me: did not these peoples struggle harder to enlarge their domains than did Your Majesties to bring the Indies under the rule of Spain?... What reasonable man could maintain that the funds invested in this enterprise are being spent in vain? I lose all reason when I hear that Your Majesties are being told that they should be collecting gold, silver, and products of great price, and when I hear that the service of Our Lord is not the first consideration. Let Your Majesties take careful note: the affair of the Indies counts for more, to my mind, than the affairs of France and Italy.

Moral considerations now follow – the colonists lead idle, useless lives:

...there is not a person who has not two or three Indians at his beck and call; hunting dogs; and, I am sorry to relate, several women, so beautiful as to be a marvel. This mode of behavior greatly displeases me and to my mind does not serve God. For this reason several devout monks would be of great help to us, more to purge the faith of the Christians than to bring that faith to the Indians. I should be sent fifty to sixty persons on each ship that arrives, and I would send back an equal number of slackers and rebels, as I now do; this is the best punishment, and the one that suits me best.

Next comes a report on the material status of the colony: the cattle imported from the mother country have multiplied; the land is beginning to produce crops and is proving fertile. But the Adelantado has long been unable to pay the wages of the colonists. The exaction of a gold-tribute from the Indians has been abandoned. A new method of showing a profit on the Indians has now become the usual practice: each colonist is alloted a certain number of natives to do manual labor (this is the origin of the *repartimiento* system, a *de facto* slavery). Columbus asks the sovereigns to sanction this state of affairs temporarily, for such time as the Crown is unable to pay the salaries of the colonists.

The negotiations with the rebels dragged on until the following spring. Columbus writes to the Sovereigns:

It was necessary for me to temporize, but I have had good reason to grow weary of this, for we are now in the month of May [1499] and each day these people bring me unpleasant surprises, and troubles. ... They never cease speaking ill of me and of this isle of Hispaniola, this land that is one of the most fertile and lovely under Heaven, full of gold, spices, brazil-wood. ... They have accused me for no just reason whatsoever, in order that Your Majesties should conceive a hatred for me, and for my enterprise; it would not have been thus had the author of the discovery been a converted Jew, one of those *conversos* who are the sworn enemies of the good fortunes of Your

Majesties. But they have slandered my work so as to ruin it.

Salvador de Madariaga translates the last sentence [Mas echaron esta fama y tuvieron forma que llegase a se perder del todo] as: "But they spread this name [of *converso*] about in such a way as to ruin everything," and considers this to be proof that Columbus was accused of being of Jewish origin. This translation does not seem satisfactory to me, either grammatically or contextually; Columbus had, in fact, just mentioned that if he had been among the number of those who were *conversos* ("as are most of the partisans of Roldán"), they would not have dared attack him.

Roldán finally managed to have the matter settled on his own terms: he was given back his title of *Alcalde Mayor*; as for his cohorts, they could either remain in the island with fine land grants or go back to the mother country.

The two ships, which had lain idle for a year (Columbus had had to give up the idea of sending them off to continue the exploration of the Gulf of Paria) set sail in the autumn of 1499 with many hidalgos aboard, each of whom was bringing back at least one Indian slave. This must have made a very bad impression on the Queen, who was in Cádiz the very moment that the human cargo was unloaded. The shipment numbered three hundred Indians, and included women and children. Up to this time the sovereigns had not been disturbed, thinking that "the right of nations" had been respected since it was a question of prisoners of war; but no letter of explanation from the Viceroy mentioning battles with the Indians had been forthcoming. Las Casas' father was among the hidalgos that had been repatriated, and the future Historian of the Indies, who witnessed the scene, reports that Isabella asked, in great anger: "Who authorized my Admiral to hand over my subjects as chattel to any person whatsoever?" And the Queen ordered that the Indians be taken back to Hispaniola.

The letters that the Viceroy had sent by the same mail did not make a favorable impression either, for they betrayed a weak man, overwhelmed by events. He com-

146

plained that his hand had been forced by Roldán, and requested that a "learned and experienced person" be sent to help him administer justice.

This aging man, feeling his undertaking about to go to pieces, was undergoing a great inner crisis. The following brief episode throws light on the anguished, mystical nature of this crisis:

On Christmas Day [1499] all had abandoned me . . . and I had come to the bitter end. I put everything aside and went aboard a little caravel. Our Lord then came to my aid, saying unto me: "Man of little faith, fear not. I am here. I shall provide for all things. The seven years set aside for the gold has not yet passed." Thus did He show me that He could rout my enemies and fulfill my every wish.

*Columbus punishes the rebels. (Théodore de Bry, Americae pars IV).*

The "seven years set aside for the gold" should be compared with a letter sent by Columbus to the Pope (in 1502):

> The affair of the Indies had as its aim the ransom of the Holy House of Jerusalem; from the moment that I found these lands, I wrote to the Sovereigns, saying that seven years hence I would give them the sum needed to pay fifty thousand foot soldiers and five thousand knights.

The "vision" of Christmas, 1499, thus clearly reveals the major obsession of this tormented man: gold, yes – but gold to guarantee the fulfillment of his mission, to be the instrument of a crusade.

Now that a peaceful settlement had been signed with Roldán, the Viceroy seemed to take command of the situation again. He distributed lands to the colonists and the Indians. The mines began to be worked again, but the gold-tribute was now strictly supervised to ensure that the Crown received its due share. This produced discontent:

> Those who had returned to Castile maintained that the Admiral was concealing the real riches of this land. They accused both him and his brothers of cruelty and incompetence. . . . If such a situation were not remedied, [they said that] the Admiral would rebel and form an alliance with a ruler who would aid him, for he claimed that everything belonged to him because he had discovered it, thanks to his skill and his pains. . . .
> [*History* of Ferdinand Columbus.]

We may readily imagine that Columbus' views were open to such a slanderous interpretation, for even on his deathbed he was to insist that he had *given* the Indies to the Kingdom of Castile, a boast that the Spaniards found intolerable. But the accusation of premeditated treason was totally unfounded, and the Admiral easily absolved himself:

> I wonder who could think me so stupid as not to understand that, even though the Indies belonged to me, I could not sustain myself therein without the aid

of a ruler; and where could I have found greater aid
than from the King and Queen, who raised me out of
nothingness to this high position, and have even taken
my sons into their service?

All these rumors stemmed from the xenophobia aroused
by the three brothers and the numerous Genoese in their
entourage. ("I beg you to bring it about that no more
people of their nation come to these islands," a Franciscan wrote to the Court.) Oviedo, the Royal Chronicler
(who later was an officer of the Crown in the Indies and
was well acquainted with the question) wisely wrote: "To
please everyone, a Governor would have to be either
angelic or superhuman."

In the spring of the year 1500 Columbus – at long
last – took stern measures. Since he had been reinstated
as Alcalde Mayor, Roldán had imposed strict discipline
in the territory of Xaraguá. One of his hidalgos had
kidnapped the daughter of a cacique and Roldán had had
him put in prison. Adrián de Moxica, the hidalgo's
cousin, had thereupon incited a band of Christians to
revolt and had threatened to kill the Viceroy and his
Alcalde. Roldán had him taken prisoner and sent him to
Columbus. Justice was promptly done: Moxica was condemned to be hanged, but refused to confess his sins
"in order to put off the fatal moment"; he was then
thrown to his death from the towers of the fortress.
Justice was severe in these times, but Columbus was
accused of great cruelty in having had Moxica put to
death before he had been able to receive the last sacraments. Other acts of cruelty ascribed to him during
the period that he had been Governor included the fact
that he had forced undernourished hidalgos to perform
manual labor, and the fact that he had hanged those of
the hidalgos who had disobeyed his orders and roamed
about the countryside foraging for food at the risk of
being massacred by the Indians. Las Casas, who arrived
in the island shortly thereafter, writes: "I have seen the
records of the trial and knew many of the witnesses
testifying against the Admiral and his brothers." He
then adds: "But no one found anything to say against
the decency of his personal conduct."

Though Columbus did not suspect it, he had been in disgrace for more than a year. The mere presence of a number of repatriated malcontents in the mother country was proof that Columbus' governorship had been a failure. As early as May 21, 1499, the Sovereigns had appointed a certain Francisco de Bobadilla, a Knight-Commander of one of the orders of chivalry, not only to the office of Royal Commissioner to arbitrate the differences between the Viceroy and Roldán, but also to the office of Governor of the island, and had provided him with a letter of credence addressed to their Admiral. But this was kept secret, and Bobadilla's departure did not take place until a year later, when suspicions concerning Columbus had been aggravated by the arrival of the two shiploads of Indian slaves. Commander Bobadilla put out to sea during the summer of 1500, and anchored off Santo Domingo on August 23. Of the three Columbus brothers, Diego was the only one then in the capital; Christopher was in Concepción and Bartholomew in Xaraguá where he was still rounding up Moxica's partisans. The first thing that Bobadilla saw was a gibbet, from which hung the corpses of six men who had been hanged. Sixteen gentlemen-rebels had, in fact, been captured by Bartholomew and sent to Santo Domingo to be put to death. The commander immediately freed those of the condemned men still in the fortress; when Diego protested, saying that he was not about to take orders from anyone but his brother, Bobadilla threw him in prison. He then set up headquarters in the Governor's mansion, impounded Columbus' records and stores of gold, and declared that he had come to discharge all arrears of pay due. Two messengers were sent to the Admiral with royal letters of credence, which contained the terse statement: "Our Commander will speak to you in our name." Protesting that the Sovereigns could not revoke his rights as Governor and Viceroy, Columbus went back to Santo Domingo with a heavy heart, and was immediately clapped in irons without so much as an interview with Bobadilla. Bartholomew was accorded the same treatment. According to Las Casas' account:

When it came time to put the Admiral in irons,

none of those who were present dared to do the deed, out of respect for his person. But a lowly cook of his household who happened to be there put them on him, with an air of shameless impudence and as much self-assurance as if he were serving him some savory dish.

Having been treated in this outrageous manner, Columbus no doubt feared the worst. One day early in the month of October an equerry came down to the cell where he was secretly imprisomed, and requested Columbus to follow him. Las Casas reports this touching scene:

"Vallejo, where are you taking me?" the Admiral asks.

"Sire, I am taking you to the ship that you are to board."

"Vallejo, is this the truth?"

"I swear it on Your Excellency's life it is true that you are going aboard ship."

These words brought him back to life.

Once the three brothers had been put aboard and the ship was on the high seas Vallejo, who no doubt disapproved of Bobadilla's odious acts, offered to take off the prisoners' chains. Columbus proudly refused, saying that he would remove them only at the Sovereigns' order. He was later to keep these chains as a memento. "I have always seen them given a place of honor in his house," his son Ferdinand writes, "and he even ordered that they be buried with him."

During the month-long crossing the Viceroy had more than enough time to reflect on his fall from grace and prepare his plea. This he did not address to the Sovereigns directly, but instead sent it to a person very close to them at court: Doña Juana de Torres, the former governess of the Infante.

This letter gives us a true likeness of Columbus, for in it his disordered thoughts are set down just as they occur to him. It is a confident appeal to the Queen, his ever-faithful protectress; as a justification of his conduct as Governor it is an amalgam of humility and pride that reproduces the whole color of his personality:

The world has ever treated men ill. It has attacked me a thousand times; until this moment I have resisted all such attacks. Today it casts me down most cruelly; but the hope in Him who created all things sustains me, for His help has been ever at hand. Once before I was downcast and He said unto me: "Man of little faith, fear not, be comforted. I am with thee." I was led to serve these rulers with utmost affection; I have indeed served them, in such great measure that the like has never before been heard. I made myself the messenger of the new Heaven and the new earth revealed by Our Lord in the *Book of the Apocalypse* through the mouth of Saint John, after the revelation through the mouth of Isaiah, and I am returning from these lands. Everyone listened to me in disbelief, but God gave unto the Queen the spirit of understanding, and high resolve; He endowed her, as a beloved daughter, with the inheritance of this whole New World. . . . Her Majesty has ever esteemed me, and sustained me to the utmost of her power. . . . For nine years I have done deeds worthy of memory. They have counted for naught. Today even the lowliest of men revile me; only the virtuous do not consent so to do. If I had taken the Indies as booty and given them unto the Moors, I should not have been shown more hatred than in Spain. . . . I have long been ready to return to Their Majesties, bringing them the glad tidings of gold, and I have long desired to flee this place so that I need no longer govern these wayward people, who fear neither their God nor their Sovereigns. Before I left Spain, I had already requested Their Majesties to appoint an official to go with me to administer justice; I again requested this following Roldán's sedition. . . . Commander Bobadilla finally arrived. From the second day he took upon himself the office of Governor, and proclaimed the suspension of the gold tax for twenty years; he announced that he intended to pay the salaries of all the colonists; that as for me and my brothers, he would have us thrown in irons – which he did – adding that neither I nor any of my family would return here, and saying of me a thousand slanderous things. . . . He ordered that inquiries be made concerning my conduct, imputing to me more iniquities than are found in Hell. But Our Lord – He who rescued Daniel and the three children from the fiery furnace – came to my aid. . . . The first thing he [Bobadilla] did was to seize my gold in my absence, saying that he wished to use it to pay the men. Of this gold I had set apart certain nuggets large as goose- or hen-eggs which certain of my men had collected within

*Vasco da Gama.*

L'Amirante Don          Vasco de Gama

a very short time, in order that I might show them to Their Majesties that they might rejoice therein. There was also a gold chain weighing twenty marks, which has not been heard of since. I had 600,000 *maravedis* and was intending to pay every person, slighting no one; I would still have had 4 million *maravedis* due from quit rents, without touching the gold. All this he has most liberally distributed: Your Majesties may judge the truth of this when they order him to present his accounts.... I was done a great injury when the person sent to investigate my conduct was a man who knew that if his report showed the facts in a bad enough light he would remain there himself as Governor.... It was to do me an injury to judge me as if I were an ordinary governor administering Sicily or some city with well-established laws and regulations. I should be judged as a captain who left Spain to go as far as the Indies, conquering as I went a populous and belligerent nation, whose customs and religion are quite the opposite of ours; I have brought this other world under the dominion of the King and Queen; and Spain, which was reckoned poor, has become rich.... I ought to be judged as a captain who has borne arms for many a year, not laying them down a single day; as a conquistador, not as a cleric.... If I have erred, it is not through evil intentions, and I believe that Their Majesties will so judge. I hold for certain that they will show me mercy, for my errors were committed unwittingly, as they will soon recognize, and will take account of my services, which will each day prove greater.

As soon as the caravels arrived in Cádiz – on October 25, 1500 – this letter was forwarded posthaste to the Court, and an order to release the prisoners arrived straightway. They were summoned to Court a month later by Ferdinand and Isabella. Las Casas reports:

The sovereigns received the Admiral and his brothers most graciously, showing compassion for their adversity, giving them all consolation that was within their power, assuring the Admiral that his imprisonment had not been by their order, promising him that all would

154

be remedied and his privileges restored; the Queen in particular took the greatest pains to console him and assure him of her regret, for it was in her that the Admiral placed all his hopes. He had fallen to his knees, sobbing and weeping, but for a moment he could not say a single word. They bade him rise, and he began his difficult and painful speech, professing his sincere love and his everlasting devotion to Their Majesties' service.

Columbus' fall from favor had nonetheless begun. Though he still enjoyed the affection and esteem of the sovereigns – or at least of the Queen – the whole of his rights and prerogatives was never restored to him. Commander Bobadilla was ordered, it is true, to return the property he had confiscated, and an agent was sent to Hispaniola to see that Columbus received the ten per cent of the profits due him. But official documents never again referred to him as Viceroy and Governor, and he never again enjoyed the right to govern the island that he had given Spain. Though he had the satisfaction of seeing his enemy Bobadilla reduced to poverty a year later, he also had the pain of seeing a replacement for the Commander appointed soon after. Then too, Columbus by 1500 was not the only discoverer, although the honor of having been the first was still his. Still his, too, was the wish to discover lands even more wondrous, to fulfill his mission as the Christ-Bearer by leading the way toward the reconquest of the Holy Land.

Before re-embarking on one last voyage of exploration to lands he hoped were full of gold, Columbus spent the entire year of 1501 in Andalusia, begging to go on another mission and dreaming of the designs of Providence. He occasionally paid a visit to the Sovereigns' residence in the Alhambra in Granada; but they were preoccupied with affairs in Italy and gave little sign of acceding to his wishes. On other occasions he went to Seville to the monastery of Las Cuevas, where he had previously spent the winter of 1497-1498. Las Cuevas, which lay on the banks of the Guadalquivir and was surrounded by lovely irrigated gardens, was praised by all travelers of the time as a corner of Paradise, "whence it is easy to turn one's thoughts to Heaven." (Some years later, Ignatius Loyola thought for a time of withdrawing from the world there.) At the monastery Columbus had found a great friend in the person of Fray Gaspar Gorricio, who became his spiritual advisor and his guide in Biblical exegesis.

This was a year of intense religious stimulation, during which Columbus' mystic bent was to grow even more evident.

Since his departure from Spain three years before, many new perspectives, both commercial and religious, had come into view. The route to the Indies via Africa had just been opened for Portugal, thanks to the great voyage of Vasco da Gama who had rounded the Cape of Good Hope, crossed the Indian Ocean, and reached Calcutta; this was the gold and spice route that Columbus had been so anxious to open via the west! Brazil was discovered in the year 1500; by virtue of its position east of the line of demarcation sovereignty was awarded to the Crown of Portugal. Navigators from Castile completed the coastal exploration that Columbus had begun in the Gulf of Paria in 1498, and reached the Gulf of Darien at the base of Central America. People were now beginning to suspect that South America was a real continent (although it was still thought to be a part of Asia), as Columbus had been the first to suggest. The world-map drawn by Juan de la Cosa in the year 1500 hinted that such was the case (and did not fall into Columbus' error of connecting Cuba to the "mainland"). But no one had sailed around the world as yet, and Columbus again took up this project which he had had to abandon in 1494 at the time of his exploration of Cuba.

The possibility of gaining a knowledge of the whole earth thus seemed close at hand in these years. Taking this fact as its point of departure, the restless mind of the Christ-Bearer erected grandiose schemes. Had not Joachim of Flores, the twelfth-century hermit saint whose works continued to exert an enormous influence until the sixteenth century, predicted that humanity was about to enter a "third age," during which the Church Visible, restored to life by a religious order (which Franciscans took to be *their* order), would bring the whole world under the rule of the Eternal Gospel? The end of the world would thus come to pass. But the "sect of Mohammed" must first, of course, disappear from the face of the earth.

This was a timely moment for Columbus to renew his efforts to promote the Great Enterprise – the reconquest of the Holy Sepulchre – which he had always closely allied with the affair of the Indies. The threat of a Turkish invasion again being imminent, Pope Alexander VI had promulgated in 1500 a papal bull urging a crusade. The Admiral seized upon this occasion to write a letter to the Holy Father (in 1502) giving him information about his past voyages and the current voyage he was promoting "for the exaltation of the Christian religion," and reminding him that "if Satan had not defeated my every effort" he would already have been in a position to furnish the Sovereigns 120 bushels of gold for the crusade.

But it was above all Ferdinand and Isabella who must be persuaded. A prophecy of Joachim of Flores (today known to be apocryphal) had long been current in the peninsula, to the effect that "he who would repair the Ark of Zion would come from Spain." Columbus did not fail to remind the Sovereigns of this prophecy.

Despite his painful ophthalmia, and with Father Gorricio's aid in the search for references, Columbus undertook in the year 1502 the task of assembling a compilation entitled *The Book of Prophecies*. (The manuscript numbering 84 pages, 14 of which have disappeared, is now preserved in the Biblioteca Colombina.) His plan was to cite from the Scriptures and from Biblical exegeses all the passages referring to "the recovery of the Holy City of Zion and the conversion of the island of the Indies and all nations." The prologue of the manuscript is in the form of a first draft of a letter addressed to Ferdinand and Isabella. As the first point in his letter, Columbus reminds the Sovereigns of his mission as Discoverer:

Our Lord opened my understanding, as if He had touched me with His own hand: I suddenly comprehended that it was possible to sail from here to the

Indies. . . . Through the success of this voyage He wished to make a miracle manifest, in order that I, and many others, might take heart insofar as that other enterprise is concerned: that of the Holy House of Zion. . . . In the affair of the Indies, neither reason, nor mathematics, nor world-maps were of any avail; it was necessary, rather, that the prophecy of Isaiah be fulfilled.

This was not the first time that Columbus had invoked Isaiah when discussing the Indies. He was doubtless thinking of the prophecies concerning the "Isles afar off," for example Isaiah LXVI, 19:

. . . and I will send those that escape of them unto the nations, to Tarshish, Pul, and Lud . . . to Tubal and Javan, to the Isles afar off, that have not heard my fame, neither have seen my glory; and they shall declare my glory among the Gentiles.

Columbus' second point: the restitution of the House of Zion to the Church. He announces that he will compile all the "authorities" who have mentioned bringing the Gospel to the whole world:

I shall confine myself to Holy Scripture and to the prophecies of those blessed persons who have spoken of them through divine revelation. It may be that Your Majesties and those to whom this document [i.e., the *Book of Prophecies*] is shown will come to reproach me, for I am not a cleric but, rather, an unlettered mariner and a simple layman. I shall reply in the words of Saint Matthew: "I thank thee, O Father . . . because thou hast hid these things from the wise and prudent, and hast revealed them unto babes." I say that the Holy Spirit is at work not only among Christians but among Jews, Moors, and men of any sect whatsoever, and not only among the wise but among the untutored as well. . . . I am a very great sinner, but the goodness and mercy of the Lord have sustained me each time that I have called unto Him, and my whole consolation is to seek to contemplate His wondrous face. . . . No person must fear to undertake a thing if it be in the name of the Lord. May Your Majesties remember that they had little money when they began the conquest of the Kingdom of Granada. Our Lord leaves the decision to be taken to the free will of each soul. It is His wish that man act freely, and He will reward him.

Third point: the end of the world is near.

Great things are coming to pass in the world: this have I learned from preaching the Gospel in so many lands in these days just past. . . . Saint Augustine says that the end of the world shall come in the seven-thousandth year after the Creation . . . there now remain but 155 years.

The Sovereigns must therefore hasten to fulfill the prophecies concerning the salvation of the whole world. These views of Columbus certainly accorded with the anti-Islamic policy of the sovereigns; they had pursued this policy in North Africa after the fall of Granada, and even on his deathbed Ferdinand displayed great concern for the reconquest of Jerusalem.

The more Columbus worked at his compilation, the more convinced he was that the restoration of the Kingdom of Christ depended on the fate of Jerusalem. All the psalms and prophets he was busy annotating do, in fact, frequently prophesy that Gentiles will one day come in great numbers to the capital of Zion. There is, for instance, this passage in Isaiah LX, 1-3:

Arise, shine, for thy light is come, and the glory of the Lord is risen upon thee. . . . And the Gentiles shall come to thy light, and kings to the brightness of thy rising.

These ecumenical views regarding the Kingdom of Israel were adopted by the Catholic Church, "the New Israel," (in the liturgy of the Epiphany in particular), and thus became part and parcel of the common body of religious beliefs. But aside from this fact, locating the triumph of Faith in the city of Jerusalem was a common tendency of Columbus' era; it was only later, with the advent of the *alumbrados* – the Illuminati – or similar Lutheran sects that this view became heretical and anti-

159

Roman. We must put ourselves back within the spiritual environment of that era. Cardinal Cisneros, a Franciscan monk who had been named head of the Church of Spain, was the first to think that Their Catholic Majesties' victory over Islam would not be complete until Jerusalem had been reconquered. In 1506 (the year that Columbus died) Cisneros persuaded King Ferdinand that he should propose a crusade to his sons-in law, the King of England and the King of Portugal. Soon, Cisneros said, the Holy Mysteries could be celebrated on the altar of the Sepulchre of Christ. Emmanuel of Portugal sent a favorable reply, adding that the Portuguese were already acting in the manner of true crusaders, as could be seen from the fact that the Indies had been opened up by Vasco da Gama. Three years later Cisneros, the architect of the seizure of Oran from the Moors, was congratulated for this fact in the following terms:

> Do not lay down your arms. Open the way to the Holy of Holies to the worshipers of Christ. The purified Holy Places shall become, according to the prophecy of Jeremiah, the joy of the whole earth.[1]

Amid such an atmosphere Columbus' constant – and completely sincere – claim that he was an envoy of God did not strike eminent ecclesiastics as exorbitant. Gorricio, the Carthusian Father, was honored to help him perfect his understanding of Holy Scriptures. We have already spoken of Fray Diego de Deza, the Dominican monk who first aided him. Another missionary of Genoese origin, Fray Giustiniani, a great scholar occupied in translating the psalter into four languages, did not hesitate to insert a long gloss on the Discoverer in the margin of Psalm XVIII. We there read:

> Columbus often said that he had been elected by God to fulfill the prophecy of these verses: Their sound is gone out through all the earth, and their words to the end of the world.

(These verses are used in the Church's Liturgy of the Apostles.) Guistiniani's gloss is a precious testimonial. . . .

---

[1]  See M. Bataillon: *Erasme et l'Espagne,* Paris, 1937; p. 56 ff.

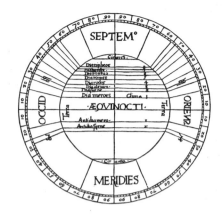

# THE LAST VOYAGE

In 1501 Columbus was fifty years old, a man now careworn and exhausted. As all men do as they grow older, he often thought back on the years of his youth, and above all else these years to him meant Genoa, his homeland. Nicolò Oderigo, the Ambassador of the Ligurian Republic to the Court of Their Catholic Majesties, became Columbus' frequent companion during his stay in Granada, and his friend and confidant. Columbus had had copies made of his *Book of Privileges* (i.e., the *Capitulations* of Santa-Fé, the entail, etc.), and two of these copies he gave to Oderigo. On April 2, 1502, Columbus wrote to the Bank of San Giorgio in Genoa:

> Although I here find myself far distant in body, my heart is ever there with you. Our Lord has granted unto me the greatest grace ever granted any man since David. The deeds that I have done now shine forth, and shall shine forth more brightly still in days to come. I shall take my departure for the Indies in the name of the Most Holy Trinity, and being mortal I have in my will instructed my son Diego to remit to you a tenth of all the revenues brought in from the Indies. . . .

161

The Bank of San Giorgio replied:

> Your glory shines forth more brightly than that of
> any man on earth, for by your perseverance, your
> courage, and your wisdom, you have brought forth
> from the depths of ignorance a vast portion of this
> earth and globe, which for all centuries past was
> unknown to men of our region.

Columbus' religious turn of mind had not dulled his
business acumen; this trait, in fact, occurs quite frequently in "visionaries" of this type. Before leaving on his
last voyage, he carefully put his papers in order and had
four notarized copies made of all the documents establishing his privileges. One of the copies went to Alonso
Sánchez de Carvajal, his agent in Hispaniola; two others
were sent, as we have seen, to Genoa; the fourth was
entrusted to Father Gorricio at the monastery of Las
Cuevas, along with the originals and a second will (now
lost) which he had drafted on April 1.

Diego, the Admiral's elder son, was now twenty years
old, and it was he who was to receive the sums to be
sent by Carvajal from the Indies. Being a good pater-
familias, Columbus left him the following instructions:

> I bid you – enjoining you so to do in the name of
> charity – to donate the tenth of your revenues to the
> needy poor, preferably to persons of our family. If
> you will so do, you shall not want, for the Lord will
> provide. I bid you to esteem and honor all persons
> having commerce with you, from the mightiest to the
> lowliest. . . . Have mercy, and know that God will
> then have mercy upon you. . . . For love of me look
> after Beatriz Enríquez as you would your mother. Let
> her receive from you 10,000 *maravedis* each year,
> over and above the sums that she receives from the
> slaughterhouses in Córdova. . . . I bid you, under pain
> of disobedience, to draw up each month an account
> of what is spent in your household and sign it, for if
> such is not done both servants and sums of money go
> astray. I bid you in all important matters to follow
> the advice of Father Gaspar [Gorricio], have him

undertake to secure a brief from His Holiness concerning my affairs [i.e., in regard to the appointment of missionaries] ... and allow him in this affair of the Indies to spend all the money necessary to propagate the Faith.

On March 14, the Admiral received orders from the Crown to sail on a voyage of exploration in the direction of the Indies. The region was not specified, but the eventuality of a meeting with Vasco da Gama in the middle of the globe was foreseen!

We are sending you a letter for the Portuguese captain who has sailed toward the East, and we inform him therein of your departure toward the West; if you meet each other en route, you are to treat each other in a friendly manner.

The Sovereigns thus approved the plan that Columbus would attempt to carry out: exploring the Indian Ocean proper (and the Golden Chersonese – the Rangoon Peninsula – which was in danger of falling into Portuguese hands) by sailing westward, beyond the already-explored "terra firma." The Admiral was also instructed not to visit Hispaniola (where Ovando, the new Governor, had just disembarked) except in case of dire necessity.

Columbus took his brother Bartholomew with him; he was also accompanied by his young son Ferdinand, just thirteen years old, who was later to record in his *History* the detailed account of the last and most harrowing of Columbus' expeditions.

The fleet of four ships, with 140 persons aboard, set sail on May 11, 1502.

The bad condition of one of his ships, the *Santiago*, forced Columbus to alter his course: hoping to exchange this ship for another sailing vessel in Hispaniola, he disregarded the Crown's orders and cast anchor off Santo Domingo on June 29, 1502. An imposing flotilla of 28 vessels lay at anchor in the roadstead. Sensing from several bad signs that a hurricane was making up, the

163

Admiral sent a request to Ovando, the new Governor, asking permission to come into harbor for shelter, and also recommended that the armada about to weigh anchor next day not be allowed to sail as planned. The Governor totally disregarded this message from the former master of Hispaniola. Ferdinand Columbus writes:

It pleased God to blind his understanding. The armada had no more than arrived at the western end of the island when a great hurricane burst upon it, swamping the flagship carrying Commander Bobadilla and the greater part of those who had rebelled against the Admiral.

Almost every one of the ships went down, losing all hands aboard and enormous sums of gold being shipped to the Crown. But three of the vessels rode it out, among them the ship carrying Carvajal, Columbus' agent, and the monies he had managed to have restored to his master. This extraordinary coincidence caused the Admiral's enemies to say that he "had produced this storm through the art of magic, in order to avenge himself." Las Casas – who had been on the scene – wrote: "The whole city of Santo Domingo, being built of wood and thatch, was laid flat, as if a whole army of demons had broken loose from Hell." As for Columbus, he had had the foresight to anchor his four caravels in the lee of a little island; though they were damaged, they managed to keep afloat through a terrifying night:

Like Job, I was on the point of perishing from despair, seeing myself forbidden entry to a land that I had won by my own sweat and blood, at a moment when I was seeking shelter to save the lives of my son, my brother, and my friends.

[Letter of Columbus.]

Early in August the caravels reached the coast of Central America, anchoring at Cape Honduras and holding a ceremony of possession there. Columbus must have been following charts of eastern and southern Asia drawn up from data provided by Marco Polo and Nicolo Conti. (G. E. Nunn [1] has attempted to reconstruct these charts by projecting on them both this imaginary track and the actual track of Columbus' last voyage.) He thought he was between *Mangi* (south China) and *Ciamba* (Annam), both of which had been mentioned by Marco Polo; following the Venetian's example, he hoped to round *Lochac* (the Malay Peninsula) so as to come upon the Malay Straits and enter the Indian Ocean bathing the shores of the Golden Chersonese (the Rangoon Peninsula).

Continual storms were to turn this exploration into a nightmare, to the point that the crew, in Columbus' words, "declared, and still declares, that we were bewitched – a heretical opinion." After a month of beating to windward they reached Cape Gracias a Dios. The coastline (of what today is Costa Rica) now trended north-and-south, and thus seemed to answer the description of the coastline of *Ciamba*.

On September 25, they anchored in the harbor of *Cariai* for a rest. The natives came aboard and offered jewels made of *guanin* in barter. They even went so far as to send two young virgins aboard as a present. Columbus, ever mindful of decorum, writes:

> [They were] seven and eleven years of age, and behaved so indecently that public women would do no better; they also brought sorceress-powders aboard; I had them clothed and sent them back ashore.

On October 5, the caravels entered the Chiriqui Lagoon; unfortunately this was not the strait they were looking for, as they were inclined at first to believe.

But another age of civilization began at this point: they now encountered not *guanin* but pure gold; the natives wore great disks of this precious metal. Thanks to his interpreters, Columbus now learned many exciting things: a great ocean (the Pacific) lay to the west, nine days' march from Chiriqui. He naturally thought that this was the Indian Ocean:

---

[1] In *Geographical Conceptions of Columbus*, New York, 1924; see above, pp. 42-43.

In the province of Ciguara which borders this sea there are, according to what these people tell me, great quantities of gold; the natives wear necklaces of coral and bracelets of gold, and cover their chests and tables with thick layers of gold; they have fairs and trading posts; the ships there are armed; the people are richly clad, and they are accustomed to waging war.

The Ganges doubtless lay only ten days' sail away!
A storm drove the vessels farther eastward, along the coast of Veragua. This time the coastline trended west-and-east (which must have surprised the explorer, for he was expecting to come upon Lochac-Malacca, but he says nothing about it). The exchange of trinkets for gold became more and more profitable. Columbus wrote to the Sovereigns:

*"It seemed like another Deluge."*

I have found more signs of gold in this land of Veragua than I found in Hispaniola in four years. The chieftains are buried, I am told, wearing their gold ornaments. . . . Josephus says in his *Antiquities* [i.e., Flavius Josephus' *Antiquities of the Jews*] that Solomon sent an expedition to look for gold in Aurea. I maintain that the mines of Aurea are these very mines of Veragua, which extends westward for a distance of more than twenty days' journey.

Columbus had previously identified King Solomon's *Ophir* with Haiti; this time he identified the Golden Chersonese with Veragua.

Still scudding before the storm, the Admiral now edged along the coast of Panama, but came to an anchor on November 26, in a well-sheltered little creek he named *Retrete* (Closet) and there took a two weeks' rest. "Having arrived there," he writes, "I changed my mind and decided to return to the mines of Veragua until the weather should permit me to continue." Search for the strait was now out of the question, not because Columbus no longer believed that it existed – as some have claimed – but rather by the force of circumstances.

As the caravels turned back, the storm again descended upon them:

Never has there been seen a sea so high, so angry, so covered with foam. The wind trapped me in this sea that had turned the color of blood, that seethed like a cauldron. The sky blazed like a fiery furnace for a day and a night. Lightning flashed in dreadful fury, and we all thought that it was about to set fire to the ships. And there was so heavy a downpour that it seemed like another Deluge.

More terrible still was a waterspout that came upon them on December 13. Ferdinand – who was still a young boy, but possessed of such courage as to arouse his father's admiration – gives this account:

This waterspout drew the water up into the clouds in a column larger than a water cask and twisted it

167

like a whirlwind. Just as it passed alongside the ships, the sailors began to recite the Gospel according to Saint John.

The Admiral drew his sword, and holding the Bible in his left hand, traced a great cross against the sky. A striking image. . . .

On January 6, Columbus anchored in a fine well-sheltered roadstead, protected from the heavy seas by a sandbar at the mouth of a river. In honor of the Feast of the Epiphany the spot was given the name *Belén* (Bethlehem) which it still bears. There they rested and attempted to repair their ships, for tropical sea worms had bored the planks completely through. Since gold was plentiful and the natives proved friendly, Columbus decided to establish a colony, as ordered in the royal instructions. His brother was to be in charge, and construction of a village was begun. But relations with the Indians deteriorated. In the month of April three of the caravels had crossed the bar and were about to take their departure, leaving the *Gallega* in the roadstead with Bartholomew in charge. Columbus had sent Captain Tristan with a boat-party to get fresh water, and he and all his party were attacked by the Indians and killed. Columbus, who had remained aboard the flagship, was worried when his men did not return. Sick with malarial fever as well, the Christ-Bearer now had a vision, which he set down in terms of grandiloquent pathos:

I had fallen asleep groaning, when suddenly I heard a most compassionate voice which said unto me: "O fool, thou man slow to believe and serve thy God, the God of every mortal! What more did He do for Moses or his servant David? Since thy birth, He hath ever cared for thee. When thou camest to an age pleasing unto Him, He made thy name to resound miraculously throughout the whole earth. He hath given the Indies unto thee, and thou gavest them to whom thou wouldst. Unto thee He hath given the keys to the gates barring the Ocean Sea, which had been locked with heavy chains. What more did He do for the nation of Israel when He led it out of Egypt? And for

168

David, whom he raised from a shepherd to a king? Turn unto him and confess thy error: His mercy is without end. Thy old age shall not keep thee from mighty deeds. Had not Abraham passed his hundredth year when He begat Isaac? The promises of God are ever fulfilled. All that He promiseth he keepeth, and more. He shall reward thee for all the perils that thou hast undergone." I heard all this within a stupor half unto death, and finding naught to say I could but weep for my errors. He who spoke ended by saying: "Fear not; have trust; all thy tribulations are written on tables of marble and are not without reason."

He could no longer think of leaving behind on these shores a colony that would surely be massacred. Three of the four caravels (the *Gallega* had been riddled by sea worms and was now useless) again put out to sea on April 16. They intended to sail back to Hispaniola as fast as possible, then set sail for Spain in new ships, for their hulls were leaking and could not go far.

The troubles of the Admiral and his company were not yet at an end. On June 25, they were shipwrecked on the north coast of Jamaica. The caravels, "pierced like honeycombs," were beached on the sand, turned into floating fortresses, and armed against possible raids.

Almost immediately after his arrival, Columbus began to compose a long letter to the Sovereigns (the same letter we have just cited at length), an incoherent account which reveals his painful, anxiety-ridden state of mind. He appeals to memories of the past, recalls the privileges they have granted him, his imprisonment, the withdrawal of his monopoly ("nowadays even tailors are granted letters patent as explorers"). He extols the territories that he has just discovered: "What has been accomplished thus far in the Indies I hold for naught by comparison with the mines that I have now brought beneath the dominion of Your Majesties." There then follows the famous eulogy of gold: "Gold is a most excellent thing. When one possesses it, one can do as he pleases in this world – thanks to gold one can even bring souls to Paradise." This is cynicism only in appearance: in Columbus' view, gold "redeems souls" only if it is employed in God's service. Before he set sail had he not ordered Diego to give a tenth of his revenues to the poor? There is, moreover, the matter of the crusade: "Jerusalem and Mount Zion must be rebuilt by Christian hands. Abbot Joachim has said that this Christian was to come from Spain." He adds: "The Emperor of Cathay long ago asked for wise men to instruct him in the Christian faith. If Our Lord takes me back to Spain, I pledge myself to take Him thither safe and sound." This suggest that Columbus was still dreaming of an alliance with a Christianized Grand Khan, and of a seizure of Islam from the rear. The letter ends with this pathetic peroration:

> I have not a single hair that is not white, and my body can bear no more. . . . May heaven have mercy upon me, and earth weep over me. Of things material, I have not so much as a copper left to give at the offertory; in things spiritual, I am alone and ill, awaiting death from day to day, surrounded by a million savages hostile to us, so far distant from the Sacraments of Our Holy Church that my soul will be damned should it part from my body. Let him who hath a sense of charity, truth, and justice weep for me. If it shall please God to deliver me from this place, I implore Your Majesties to grant me permission to go to Rome and other pilgrim-shrines!

The Admiral fortunately found a valuable aide: the hidalgo Diego Méndez, an exemplary Castilian caballero whose loyalty and bold courage stood every test. Méndez was able to win the Indians' good will, and they promised to come regularly to provision the shipwrecked men in return for the Christians' highly prized trinkets. On July 7, Diego volunteered for the perilous mission of paddling a simple dugout canoe as far as Santo Domingo to get a rescue ship. He accomplished this heroic feat, but once he arrived in Hispaniola it took him eight months to charter a vessel.

Since no news arrived before March, 1504, the shipwrecked men thought that everyone had abandoned them. The Admiral was confined to his bed by an attack of arthritis. The inactivity made the men restless. The

170

Porras brothers (one of whom was Crown Comptroller of the expedition, the other Captain of a caravel) claimed that Columbus was staying in Jamaica on purpose, out of fear that he would be exiled if he returned to Spain; this was their way of gaining the support of the malcontents. On January 2, 1504, there occurred a dramatic scene, reported by both Ferdinand and Las Casas: a band of about fifty conspirators, all armed, climbed up to the poopdeck of the vessel and rushed into the cabin where Columbus, who was still ill, was lying in bed. Francisco de Porras confronted him with this question: "Sir, why do you refuse to return to Castile? Do you wish to see us all perish here?" Columbus replied: "You see that it

*Columbus' cabin (reconstruction). (Museo Naval, Madrid).*

is impossible for us to begin the homeward crossing until Méndez sends us a ship to sail in. As God is my witness, I wish this more than any of you, for I am duty-bound to account to God and to the Sovereigns for each one of you." Porras then left, shouting: "Let those of you who choose to go to Castile follow me!" This band of men then deserted; they failed, however, in their attempts to leave the island in dugout canoes, and settled in another part of the island.

The situation with the Indians was also precarious: the supply of trinkets was dwindling, and they were growing tired of bringing cassava bread each day. Columbus now thought up a stratagem in the grand manner. Having consulted an astronomical almanac (the *Ephemerides* of Abraham Zacuto, Columbus' copy of which has come down to us), he knew that an eclipse of the moon was due on the night of February 29, 1504. He arranged a meeting of all the neighboring caciques for that night, and preached a sermon: the God of Heaven stood ready to punish them for their ill will toward the Christians and would send them a sign that very night: the moon would disappear. The lunar disk began, indeed, to grow smaller, and the terrified Indians begged this white man to intercede with his God. Being a perfect actor, Columbus retired to his cabin, calmly measured the duration of the eclipse by his hourglass (which also allowed him to make a calculation of longitude that for once was very nearly accurate), and when he saw that the eclipse was almost over, he again came out and assured the Indians that God's wrath would be appeased if they would promise to provide food for the Christians. At that moment the moon reappeared. . . . The effect was naturally overwhelming.

In March a small caravel sent by Governor Ovando arrived at last; although it was not large enough to repatriate all the shipwrecked men, it did bring a message from Méndez to the effect that he would soon be in a position to send a rescue ship. The Admiral magnanimously sent a message to the rebels informing them of this approaching event. They proved so arrogant that a pitched battle resulted. Columbus, who was defeated in the battle, then signed a general amnesty. On June 29,

1504, a year after the ships had been beached, a caravel brought the entire company back to Santo Domingo. The former Governor of Hispaniola received the barest official welcome on the part of Ovando, who had made almost no effort to send him aid. The Admiral went back to Spain as soon as possible, in the company of his brother and his son, who had both stood the test so valiantly. On November 7, he disembarked at Sanlúcar. He was never again to see the "Indies."

Columbus now had but a year and a half to live. We must abandon the romantic image – which so seduced Léon Bloy and Claudel – of a man of genius who died unrecognized, neglected, and poverty-stricken. Until the very end the Admiral was to have faithful friends, some of them important personages. And he received large sums from the revenues that came in from the Indies, though admittedly these were paid only in part, after long delay.

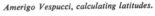

*Amerigo Vespucci, calculating latitudes.*

What is pathetic is to see Columbus struggle month after month, despite his waning strength, for the full restitution of his rights. We know that the Sovereigns had written him, just before he sailed on the last voyage:

> The favors that we have granted you shall be maintained in their entirety, according to the form and tenor of your privileges; you and your children shall enjoy them, as is right and just, and we shall order your son to be put in full possession of them.

Columbus had carefully put this letter in the hands of Fray Gorricio, who was keeping his papers for him in Las Cuevas. Columbus' son Diego was living at court, for he had been appointed to the Queen's household; the sovereigns had been planning for more than two years to unite a young girl of noble family, the niece of the Duchess of Alba, and this future admiral in marriage. (The marriage took place in 1508.)

Because he was too ill to travel to the Sovereigns' court in the distant city of Medina del Campo, Columbus took up residence in Seville and sent his brother Bartholomew and his son Ferdinand to court. He writes to Diego:

> Treat your brother with great respect. He has a naturally kind heart and is no longer a child. Ten brothers would be none too many. I have never found better friends than my brothers.

He also urged his heir to remain at court to "plead our cause."

He had been in Spain only three weeks when Queen Isabella died on November 26, at the age of fifty-three – the same age as Columbus. Upon learning of her death, Columbus expressed regret at "news so contrary to that which my soul desires." "But," he added, "the Queen is now far from this bitter and wearisome world!" For some time he entertained hopes that the Queen had mentioned him in her will and had ordered him put back "in possession of the Indies." These hopes were not fulfilled.

174

Until the spring of 1505 his *gota* – the creeping arthritis he was suffering from – grew more and more severe. He wrote letter after letter to Diego: He was to press the King for payment of the wages of his crew, "for these men are poor; they have suffered unbelievable hardships." He was to call the King's attention to a copy of a letter of 1502 promising the Admiral that all his privileges would be restored. Ferdinand was to urge Governor Ovando to send Columbus the sums owed him. Columbus, a sharp businessman who kept careful accounts, wrote: "These must amount to seven or eight thousand pesos."

There were emissaries who went to Medina del Campo on Columbus' behalf: both his faithful friend Diego Méndez and (in February, 1502) Amerigo Vespucci, "who has always shown himself eager to please me; he is an honorable man whom Fortune has not favored until now." (The Genoese and the Florentine had probably met in Seville in the house of Gianno to Berardi, who had provided capital for the expeditions of both men. At this juncture Columbus could hardly have suspected that Vespucci would publish an account of his voyage to Paria to which he assigned a date two years previous to the actual composition in order to rob Columbus of his claim to prior discovery; nor could he have suspected that this account would enjoy such success that the name *America* would make its appearance on a chart in the year 1508!)

From this correspondence between Columbus and his son we learn in passing that the new Pope, Julius II (a Genoese), "complains that I have not written to him." He therefore hastened to send the Holy Father an account of his voyage, and forwarded a copy of it to his old friend Diego de Deza, the Dominican monk who had just been named Archbishop of Seville. This account is indeed a glorious one. . . .

When fine weather returned, Columbus at last had enough strength to travel, thanks to the fact that permission had been granted him to ride a mule – a privilege ordinarily enjoyed only by ecclesiastics and women. He journeyed to Segovia, where the Sovereigns were holding court, and there enjoyed a happy family reunion with

175

his brothers and his two sons; he also had the satisfaction of receiving, little by little, the money owed him, for his friend Deza, the Archbishop and executor of the Queen's will, saw to it that the monetary obligations of the deceased Sovereign were fulfilled.

Naturally the Admiral's first duty was to go to kiss the hands of the King, who was holding court in the Alcazar, the lovely royal palace in Segovia. Ferdinand was cordial but uncommunicative. On the question of the hereditary rights of Columbus, he proposed that Deza act as arbitrator. Columbus stubbornly refused, and wrote the King:

> Most eminent Prince, through a miracle Our Lord sent me to this country to serve Your Majesty; I say through a miracle because I was for fourteen years unable to reach the ear of the King of Portugal. . . . Your Majesty graciously accorded me honors and titles. Now that my undertaking is growing ever larger, there is reason to believe that Your Majesty will renew the favors promised me by his word and seal. May Your Majesty be certain that if such is done, I shall continue to serve the Crown for the few days I have left to live. I put my hope in Divine Grace, and I am convinced that my deeds will shine a hundred times more splendidly than they have up to the present.

But it was due to the very fact that the discovery made in the Indies had taken on unexpected proportions that the King had no intention of restoring his Admiral's pecuniary and governmental rights over all territory lying west of the line of demarcation – as had been imprudently set forth in the document of April 30, 1493, shortly after its discovery.

Until the very end Columbus was to nourish the hope that his son, at least, would regain possession of all the rights due him. Many of the people close to him shared this conviction, at least insofar as the government of Hispaniola was concerned. The ever-faithful Diego Méndez thus writes:

> One day when His Lordship the Admiral was in Salamanca, lying abed because of his arthritis, I went

176

to see him and said to him: "Your Lordship knows full well the many things I have done in his service. . . . I therefore ask Your Lordship to grant me some reward." The Admiral answered me with a smile, saying that I should tell him what I wished. I then begged him to grant me the office of Chief Constable in the island of Hispaniola for my lifetime. He told me that he would grant me this willingly, and that it was small reward for my services. He asked me to tell this to his son Diego, who was most pleased and said that if his father gave me this office with one hand, he gave it to me with two hands.

In 1508 Diego's tenacity overcame the Crown's resistance and the "Second Admiral" became Governor of Hispaniola. But Christopher did not have the joy of witnessing this during his lifetime. After many fruitless petitions he wrote these sage words to Archbishop Deza:

Since it is patent that His Majesty does not wish to keep the promise made me, by his word and seal, I think that continuing the battle would be like contending with the wind; since I have done everything within my power, it is best that I now commend myself to Our Lord, who hath ever shown Himself prompt to aid me.

Three weeks before his death Columbus made one last effort. Learning that the Sovereigns' daughter, the Infanta Juana ("la Loca"), was arriving in Flanders to succeed her mother on the throne of Castile, Columbus sent his brother Bartholomew to the Infanta with this message:

Although I am mercilessly racked with illness, I would still be able to render Your Highness unheard-of services. . . . I beg Your Highness most humbly to believe in my good will, hoping that I shall again be granted the honors due me by the terms of the instruments of privilege in my possession.

On May 19, 1506, Columbus' illness grew suddenly worse during a stay in Valladolid in the company of his sons, his brother Diego, and two faithful friends of the days in Jamaica – Diego Méndez and Bartolomeo Fieschi, a Genoese. (These surroundings bore no resemblance to the miserable little inn that became a literary commonplace.) He now sent for a notary and placed in his hands the will that he had had drawn up in Seville the year before – this document in turn being merely a codicil to the will of 1502, which has unfortunately been lost. The will was then read aloud by the notary, at the request of "Don Cristóbal Colón, Admiral, Viceroy, and Governor of the islands and mainland of the Indies, discovered and to be discovered, titles which he hereby swears are his" (note the magnificent obsession of this dying man). The will opens with a proud preamble:

When I came to serve the King and Queen by discovering the Indies – it would be more exact to say that I *gave* them the Indies by the will of God, for I long importuned them to undertake this affair, which was completely ignored and unknown to all those consulted thereupon – Their Majesties provided no more than a million *maravedis* and the burden of the rest fell upon me; Their Majesties therefore granted me permission to share in the revenues of the said Indies, beyond a line that runs one hundred leagues westward of the Azores and Cape Verde from pole to pole, as can be seen at greater length in my letters of privilege.

The principal clauses of the will were as follows: The entail settled on his elder son and heir, Diego, was confirmed. Diego was enjoined to give a share of his revenues to poor relatives, and other shares were to go to his young brother and his uncles. There was a special clause concerning Beatriz Enríquez: "I order my son Diego to provide the necessary funds for her to live a comfortable life. May he so do in order to unburden my conscience, for this matter weighs heavily upon my soul. It is not seemly that I write herein the reason thereof." Diego was to provide funds for an ecclesiastical living for three chaplains, who were each to offer a daily mass: "a votive mass in honor of the Holy Trinity, another in honor or the Conception of Our Lady, and a Requiem

178

for my soul and the souls of my father, my mother, and my wife." If possible, these masses were to be instituted somewhere in Hispaniola, "which God gave me through a miracle; I should wish particularly that this be in the place called Concepción de la Vega, where I once invoked the Holy Trinity. (Were it not for this clause, we would not know of this episode.)

The will was accompanied by a memorandum, also in Columbus' hand, listing the names of certain persons to whom Columbus owed money; Diego was to pay these debts "without these persons knowing whence the money has come." These creditors were all Genoese living in Lisbon (notably heirs of Paolo di Negro and Luigi Centurione).

The following day, May 20, 1506, the vigil of the Feast of the Ascension – a fitting liturgical coincidence! – Columbus asked to see a priest. A Franciscan friar brought him the last sacraments and administered extreme unction. The Christ-Bearer undoubtedly was clad in his habit of the Third Order of Saint Francis. Conscious to the end, he joined in the prayers for the dying, repeating with his last breath the words of Christ: *In manus tuas, Domine, commendo spiritum meum.*

His body was first buried in the Franciscan monastery of the city; three years later, by Diego's order, it was transferred to the monastery of Las Cuevas, where Columbus had found so much aid and enlightenment. In 1541 the body was removed to the cathedral of Santo Domingo, on that island of Hispaniola that the Admiral had always considered his own. His remains are there still, though they were presumably twice disinterred – once to transfer them to Cuba, and later to bring them back to Seville. We now know, however, that the body disinterred was that of the "Second Admiral," Columbus' son Diego.

During the entire sixteenth century the official chronicles of the Spanish Court were deliberately slanted in Columbus' disfavor, as a result of the endless litigation involving the heirs of Columbus and the Crown.[1] His

---

1 On this subject see Marcel Bataillon. *L'entreprise de Colomb défigurée sous Charles Quint,* Institut de France, 1954.

detractors either attempted on the one hand to deny Columbus all credit for conceiving the project and carrying it out, or on the other hand tried to claim that he had had only the discovery of a few islands, not that of the Indies, in mind. These prejudices have passed into modern criticism, born in the nineteenth century before Las Casas' *History of the Indies* was known; and it is now difficult to rid Columbus' person of a certain aura of charlatanism that has come to surround his name. He may certainly be accused of imaginatively amplifying the facts, but the more intimately we come to know him, the more we appreciate his perfect sincerity.

In conclusion, let us re-examine the two titles of glory that Columbus would have asked posterity to grant him: the Discoverer, the Christ-Bearer.

He was indeed a discoverer, but he was not a conqueror or a builder. "I ought to be judged as a knight of conquest, not as an administrator," he wrote in his appeal of the year 1500. A conquering knight, yes – in the manner of a Don Quixote, rather than that of those conquistadores who were to swoop down on the Americas "like a flight of hawks," intrepid and cruel.

He was indeed courageous and long-suffering – but only when at sea. He was fully master of himself and his men only when he was on the bridge of his ship. As we have seen, on Christmas Day, 1499, driven to despair by the ingratitude of his men, he put his duties as Viceroy aside and went aboard "a little caravel" to find peace and solitude. On land he had neither the audacity of a Cortez, who marched to the capital of Mexico after he had been cut off from his bases and his ships had been burned, nor that of a Pizarro, who with only 180 men attacked the Andes and the empire of the Incas. Columbus took off on no gigantic military expeditions, incurred no superhuman risks. The pitched battles he was obliged to wage with the Indians in Haiti were not particularly dangerous, and it would seem that he himself never once buckled on his cuirass to do battle.

From the moment that he landed anywhere, his one thought was to sail off again, to "exercise the appetite and inclination that God had given him," as Las Casas put it, to discover more and more new lands. It was when he was conning his caravel, when he put ashore at some promontory to erect a great cross, when he recorded the day's adventures and expectations each evening in his ship's log, that he was truly himself – a keen observer and a lyric visionary.

The title closest to his heart, the title he enjoined his heir to adopt as his only signature, was that of *Admiral*.

*Admiral of the Ocean Sea:* more than any other, this was the title that he had stubbornly insisted that the Sovereigns grant him should he succeed. To a sailor and a Genoese, this must have meant a great deal. There had been a line of Genoese admirals in Castile – the Boccane-

*Claudel's* Christopher Columbus, *as portrayed by Jean-Louis Barrault.*

gras – and another in Portugal – the Pessanhos. And let us not forget Columbus' mysterious phrase: "I am not the first admiral in my family. . . ." The title of Admiral made him the equal of the Admiral of Castile, the uncle of Ferdinand the Catholic. His jurisdiction was to begin where that of the Admiral of Castile left off – beyond the Azores-Cape Verde meridian – and was to include the right to a percentage of the profits on cargoes and trade of any ship entering his waters.

One cannot imagine a landbound Columbus, leading the life of the Spanish colonists he settled in Haiti, at work in their fields and mines, surrounded by their Indian laborers; nor can one imagine him a builder of cities such as Pizarro, who came to have a deep affection for the city of Lima, his new capital. Columbus had no ties, no roots. The hidalgos had nothing but scorn for the Admiral, Las Casas says, because he had no feudal estate in Spain. In 1497 he refused the fief that the Sovereigns offered him in Hispaniola, "because everyone would say that I set aside the best lands for myself," – or so he claimed; it is more likely that his real reason was that the offer hardly tempted him. (He would no doubt have cursed his grandson Luis for agreeing to give up the Viceroyalty of the Indies in return for a duchy in Veragua.)

If the "Discoverer" was great, the "Christ-Bearer" failed, for the time being at least. It is all too obvious that the treatment to which the Indians were subjected – "pacification" by armed troops, forced labor, not to mention enslavement pure and simple – frustrated the effort to convert them, the primary and official aim of the discovery. Yet Columbus understood and extolled the inherent virtues of the Indians – the gentleness and generosity that made them worthy Christian converts; he was interested in their religious customs, and concluded that they believed in a God who created and a God who avenged. He encouraged Fray Ramón Pane in his apostolic mission, and was rightly disturbed when other missionaries did not arrive. He took steps to obtain from Alexander VI, and later Julius II, the power to appoint missionaries directly, and mentioned this question once again in his last will and testament.

This was not an idle concern. The clause in his will of 1498 requesting the endowment of four chairs for doctors in theology to convert the Indians was respected by his son and successor; Diego established the Seminary of Santo Domingo, and from this institution came Montesinos, a celebrated Dominican missionary who in a ringing sermon in 1511 proclaimed the Indians' right to freedom. This was the beginning of the struggle for justice to which Las Casas was to devote his entire life.

As we have seen, Columbus took the mission of Christ-Bearer in an even larger sense. Claudel has called him "the Reassembler of God's earth," and Léon Bloy gave him the glorious title of "Revealer of the Globe." He was indeed these. He considered himself a latter-day apostle, and sailed off to bring the Grand Khan the Glad Tidings of the Gospel and an alliance with the Christians, contributing thus to the reconquest of the Holy Sepulchre and a renaissance of the Church centering in its own cradle: Jerusalem. It is true that his geographical conceptions of how close the Indies lay led him astray. He never knew that he had "discovered America," for he was firmly convinced that his New World touched the Ancient World, was one with it. When he landed in South America, there came to him for an instant the presentiment of the total newness of this other world – "a world unknown to the ancients" – but he thought that it lay in the approximate latitude of Australia in relation to Asia, and thought that it was separated from the "mainland" of Cuba by a strait, which he made a desperate attempt to find in 1503. Had he lived until 1522, he would have seen Magellan's expedition realize his dream of sailing around the world and would then have come to understand the actual dimensions of the globe.

The alliance with the Grand Khan was a medieval dream, yet it was a fruitful one. It was not Cathay that Cortez reached in 1519; he marched, rather, into the very heart of the Aztec empire. How Columbus would have rejoiced to see an immense pagan empire fall within the orbit of Christendom! He would certainly have shared the illusions of the Franciscan missionaries who sailed off in high enthusiasm to found what they thought would be a latter-day Kingdom of Christ, to renew the

183

Acts of the Apostles. With the fall of the Inca empire in 1532, the territory under Spanish rule was again enlarged. Fifty years after Columbus' death the Spanish Viceroyalties extended from Mexico in the north to Chile in the south, and the cross had been planted everywhere. The story of this victory, whose price was violence, is a sad one, but it has its counterpart in the proclamation of true Christian principles by Las Casas and his disciples, and in the elaboration of the "Laws of the Indies" for the protection of the natives.

It is because Columbus laid these foundations for the future, in the temporal realm and in the spiritual, that his image takes on a truly prophetic dimension.

*Memorial to Columbus erected at Puntal del Sebo (Huelva).*

| | | |
|---|---|---|
| 1451 | Birth of Columbus | Birth of Isabella the Catholic |
| | | Birth of Amerigo Vespucci |
| 1452 | | Birth of Leonardo da Vinci |
| | | Birth of Savonarola |
| 1453 | | End of the Hundred Years' War |
| | | Capture of Constantinople by the Turks |
| 1454 | | Gutenberg Bible |
| 1459 | | Map of Fra Mauro |
| 1460 | | Death of Prince Henry the Navigator |
| 1461 | | Accession of Louis XI to the throne of France |
| 1469 | | Marriage of Ferdinand of Aragon and Isabella of Castile |
| 1474 | Columbus' commercial voyage to Chios | Accession of Isabella the Catholic to the throne |
| 1476 | Shipwreck off the coast of Portugal | |
| 1477 | Voyage to Iceland | |
| 1479 | Marriage? | Treaty of Alcobaças |
| 1481 | | Accession of John II to the throne of Portugal |
| 1482 | | Diego Cão arrives at the mouth of the Congo |
| 1483 | | Accession of Charles VIII to the throne of France |
| 1485 | Arrival in Spain | |
| 1486 | First interview with Ferdinand and Isabella | Fall of Malaga |
| 1487 | | Cape of Good Hope reached by Bartholomeu Dias |
| 1488 | Birth of Ferdinand Columbus at Cordova | |
| 1491 | Bartholomew Columbus in France | Birth of Ignatius Loyola |
| 1492 | | *January 2:* Fall of Granada |
| | | *March 31:* Edict expelling the Jews from Spain |
| | *April 17:* Capitulation of Santa Fé | |
| | *August 3:* Embarkation at Palos, first voyage | |

185

*September 9:* Departure from the Canaries

*October 12:* Landing at San Salvador in the Antilles

Portuguese mission in Abyssinia

*October 28:* Discovery of Cuba

Martin Behaim's terrestrial globe constructed

*December 6:* Discovery of Haiti

*December 24: Santa María* grounded

Accession of Alexander VI to Papal throne

Death of Lorenzo the Magnificent in Florence

1493    *March 4:* Return to Palos

*May 2:* Papal Bull, *Inter caeterae,* promulgated by Alexander VI

*September 25:* Embarkation, second voyage

*November 12-15:* Discovery of the Lesser Antilles

1494    *May-September:* Exploration of Cuba

*June 7:* Treaty of Tordesillas

Accession of Manuel to throne of Portugal

Savonarola master of Florence

Arrival of Charles VIII of France in Naples

1496    *June 11:* Return to Cádiz
1497

*April 3:* Marriage of the Infante Juan, heir to the throne of Castile

*April 23:* Authorization granted Columbus to establish an entail

1498    *February:* First will (act of entailment)

Accession of Louis XII to throne of France

*May 30:* Embarkation, third voyage

Cape of Good Hope rounded by Vasco da Gama

*August 4:* Gulf of Paria entered

Dürer's *Apocalypse*

*August 31:* Return to Haiti
1499    Rebellion of Roldán

Arrival of Louis XII of France in Milan

Exploration of Venezuela by Hojeda, Juan de la Cosa, and Vespucci

1500    *August 23:* Arrival of Bobadilla in Santo Domingo

Discovery of Brazil by Cabral; claimed for Portugal

| | | |
|---|---|---|
| | *November 25:* Return of Columbus to Cádiz in irons | Invasion of Europe by the Turks; crusade preached by the Pope |
| | *December 17:* Columbus received in Granada by the Sovereigns | Birth of Charles V of Spain |
| | | Death of Savonarola |
| | | Erasmus' *Adages* |
| | | Luther at Erfurt |
| | | World-map of Juan de la Cosa |
| 1501 | Composition of *Book of Prophecies* begun | *January 1:* Amerigo Vespucci arrives at Rio de Janeiro |
| 1502 | *February:* Letter to Alexander VI | *February:* Departure of Ovando for Haiti to act as governor |
| | *April 1:* Second will | |
| | *April 2:* Letter to Bank of San Giorgio in Genoa | Vasco da Gama sets out for the Indies |
| | *May 11:* Embarkation, last voyage | |
| | *August:* Ceremony of possession at Cape Honduras, Central America | |
| 1503 | *January 6:* Anchorage at Belén (Panama) | |
| | *June 25:* Shipwreck in Jamaica | Arrival of Albuquerque in the Indies |
| | | Establishment of the *Casa de Contratación* in Seville |
| | | Accession of Julius II to Papal throne |
| 1504 | *March:* Return of Columbus to Santo Domingo | Spanish victory in Italy |
| | *November 7:* Return to San Lúcar de Barrameda | *November 26:* Death of Isabella |
| | Winter in Seville | Vespucci's account of the *Mundus Novus* [New World] |
| 1505 | *May:* Segovia | Fall of Ceylon and Hormuz into Portuguese hands |
| | Third will | |
| 1506 | *May 20:* Death of Columbus in Valladolid | Michelangelo in Rome |
| | | Bramante's cupola for Saint Peter's begun |
| | | Death of Martin Behaim |
| | | Treaty of Tordesillas ratified by Julius II |

*The arrival in the "Indies." (Incunabulum, 1494, Bibliothèque Nationale, Paris)*

# BIBLIOGRAPHY

A. *Source materials not available in English:*

Bernáldez, Andrés: *Historia de los reyes católicos.* Madrid, 1878. (Biblioteca de autores españoles, t. 120)

Columbus, Christopher: *Libro de los privilegios del'almirante Don Christóbal Colón* (1498). [Ed. por Ciriaca Pérez Bustamante.] Madrid, Real Academia de la Historia, 1951.

————: Los cuatro viajes del almirante y su testamento. Edición y prólogo de Ignacio B. Anzoátegui. Buenos Aires, Espasa-Calpe Argentina, 1946. (Colección Austral, 633)

Fernández Duro, Cesareo [*ed.*]: *Pleitos de Colón.* 2 vols. Madrid, Rivadenyra, 1892-1894. (Colección de Documentos Inéditos... 2. ser. de Ultramar, t. 7-8)

ITALY. Commissione colombiana. *Raccolta di documenti e studi...* Roma, Ministero della Pubblica Istruzione, 1892-1896. [6 parts in 15 vols.]

Las Casas, Bartolomé de: *Historia de las Indias.* 5 vols [facsim.]. Madrid, 1875-1876. (Collección de Documentos Inéditos para la Historia de España, t. 62-66)

Navarrete, Martín Fernández de: *Collección de los viajes y descubrimientos que hicieron... los españoles...* 2 vols. Madrid, Imprenta Real, 1825-1837.

————: *Obras.* Ed. y estudio preliminar de Carlos Seco Serrano. Madrid, Ediciones Atlas, 1954-1955. (Biblioteca de autores españoles, t. 75-77. T. I-III: *Colección de viajes*) [A modern edition of above]

Oviedo y Valdés, Gonzalo Fernández de: *Historia general de las Indias.* Sevilla, Juam Cromberger, 1535. [First edition]

————: *Historia general de las Indias.* [Ed. por José Amador de los Rios] Madrid, Imprenta de la Real Academia de la Historia, 1851-1855. 3 parts in 4 vols. [A more recent edition of above]

B. *Source materials translated into English:*

Bourne, Edward Gaylord [*ed.*]: *The voyages of Columbus and of John Cabot.* New York, Scribner's, 1925. (Original Narratives of Early American History)

Columbus, Christopher: *The authentic letters of Columbus.* [Edited by] William Eleroy Curtis... Chicago, May, 1895. (Field Museum of Natural History, Publications, 2. [Historical series] v. 1, no. 2)

————: *The log of Christopher Columbus's first voyage to America in the year 1492, as copied out... by Bartholomew las Casas...* New York, W. R. Scott, 1938. [Another ed.]: London, W. H. Allen, 1944.

189

Columbus, Ferdinand: *The life of the Admiral Christopher Columbus by his son Ferdinand.* Translated and annotated by Benjamin Keen. New Brunswick (N. J.), Rutgers University Press, 1959.

Jane, Lionel Cecil [*ed.*]: *Select documents illustrating the four voyages of Columbus.* Translated and edited with additional material, introduction and notes. London, Hakluyt Society, 1930.

Lawrence, Arnold Walter and Jean Young [*eds.*]: *Narratives of the discovery of America.* New York, J. Cape and H. Smith, 1931.

C. *Standard studies of Columbus in English:*

Aulaire, Ingri (Mortenson) d': *Columbus.* Garden City (N. Y.), Doubleday, 1955.

André, Marius: *Columbus:* Translated from the French by Eloise Parkhurst Huguenin. New York and London, Knopf, 1928.

Hevesy, André de: *The discoverer.* Translated from the French by Robert M. Coates. New York, Macaulay, 1928.

Jane, Cecil: *Voyages of Columbus.* London, Argonaut Press, 1930.

Kimble, George Herbert: *Geography in the Middle Ages.* London, Methuen, 1938.

Link, Edwin Albert and Marion A.: *A new theory on Columbus' voyage through the Bahamas.* Washington, Smithsonian Institute, 1958. (Smithsonian Miscellaneous Collections, v. 135, no. 4)

Madariaga, Salvador de: *Christopher Columbus.* London, Hodder and Stoughton, 1939. [Another ed.]: New York, Macmillan, 1940.

Markham, C. R.: *Life of Christopher Columbus.* London, n. p., 1882.

Morison, Samuel Eliot: *Admiral of the Ocean Sea.* 2 vols. Boston, Little Brown, 1942. [Another edition, in 1 vol. without notes]: Little Brown, 1942.

————: *Christopher Columbus, mariner.* Boston, Little Brown, 1955.

————: *The second voyage of Christopher Columbus.* Oxford, Clarendon Press, 1939.

Nunn, George E.: *The geographical conceptions of Columbus.* New York, American Geographical Society, 1924.

————: "The *Imago mundi* and Columbus" *in American Historical Review* (Richmond, Va.), v. 40 (1935), pp. 646-661.

Roselly de Lorgues, Antoine François Félix: *The life of Christopher Columbus.* Compiled from the French ... by J. J. Barry, M. D. Boston, P. Donohue; New York, American News Co., 1869.

Tarducci, Francesco: *The life of Christopher Columbus.* Translated from the Italian by H. F. Brownson. Detroit, n. p., 1890.

Vignaud, Henri: *Toscanelli and Columbus... a critical study*. London, Sands, 1902.

Wassermann, Jakob: *Christopher Columbus: Don Quixote of the seas*. Translated from the German by Eric Sutton. London, Secker, 1930.


D. *Bibliography*

CONVEGNO INTERNAZIONALE DI STUDI COLOMBIANI, Genoa, 1951: *Studi colombiani*. 3 vols. Genova, Stabilimento arti grafiche ed affini, 1952. (Pubblicazioni del Civico Instituto Colombiano, Genova)

Nowell, Charles E.: "The Columbus question" *in American Historical Review* (Richmond, Va.), v. 44 (1939), pp. 802-822.

UNITED STATES. Library of Congress. Division of Bibliography: *Christopher Columbus*. A selected list of books and articles by American authors as published in America, 1892-1950. Compiled by Donald H. Mugridge. Washington, 1950.

E. *Iconography*

GENOA (*city*): *Mostra colombiana internazionale*, 1950-1951. Elenco ilustrativo a cura di Paolo Revelli. Genova, Comitato Cittadino per le Celebrazioni Colombiane, 1950.

# ACKNOWLEDGMENTS

Italian Tourist Office: p. 4. Spanish Tourist Office: p. 36. Bibliothèque Nationale (Éditions du Seuil): pp. 5, 13, 15, 16, 19, 20, 23, 24, 25, 29, 30, 34, 57, 65, 70, 71, 77, 105, 106, 107, 109, 121, 122, 134, 135, 141, 147, 161, 166. Giraudon: pp. 44, 50, 153, 173. Studio Bernard: p. 181.

Illustrations for chapter headings are taken from Ebner manuscript of Ptolemy's *Geography* (1460), reproduced from the edition of E. L. Stevenson, *Geography of Ptolemy*, New York, 1932.

P. 15: Portulan (1 meter high) attributed to Columbus (from Charles de la Roncière: *La carte de Christophe Colomb;* Paris, 1924. Posterior to January, 1492 (Granada is shown in a vignette). Principal outposts of Portuguese commerce.

P. 24: "Thyle seu Thule" is shown at 63° north latitude (as in the copy of the 1478 edition of Ptolemy owned by Columbus).

Pp. 42-43: chart by G. E. Nunn, in *Geographical Concepts of Columbus,* copyright 1924 by the American Geographical Society of New York, reproduced by permission.

P. 57: Portrait of Columbus, commissioned by the humanist Giove, which hung in his gallery — from 1537 on, at least. Conforms with descriptions of contemporaries and with the characteristics of Columbus' skull, exhumed in 1945. (See A. A. Pedroso, "El verdadero retrato de Colón" ["The true portrait of Columbus"] in *Studi Colombiani,* III, p. 25 ff.

P. 65: By an unknown Italian artist. Drawn on the copy of the *Book of Privileges* sent by Columbus to Oderigo. Allegorical figures: Providence, at Columbus' side; Religion, holding a cross and pushing the boat.

Pp. 23, 70, 188: Woodcuts of an incunabulum (incipit: De insulis in mare indico nuper repertis [i.e. a manuscript bearing the notation: "Here begins 'I report on islands in the ocean which have recently been discovered' "]) — the Latin translation of Columbus' letter announcing his discovery.

P. 191: Chief: royal arms of Castille and Aragon; dexter point: archipelago; sinister point: azure field with 5 anchors.